SOLDIER'S GUIDE
TO
A COLLEGE DEGREE

SOLDIER'S GUIDE TO A COLLEGE DEGREE

LARRY J. ANDERSON

STACKPOLE
BOOKS

Published by
STACKPOLE BOOKS
5067 Ritter Road
Mechanicsburg, PA 17055

Printed in the United States of America

10 9 8 7 6 5 4 3 2 1

First Edition

Cover design by Wendy Reynolds

Library of Congress Cataloging-in-Publication Data

Anderson, Larry J., 1968–
    Soldier's guide to a college degree / Larry J. Anderson.
        p. cm.
    Includes index.
    ISBN 0-8117-2929-X
    1. Soldiers—Education, Non-military—United States. 2. College credits—United States. 3. Degrees, Academic—United States.
    I. Title.
    U716.A68   1998
    378.2' 088355—dc21

                                                      97-42004
                                                      CIP

Contents

Preface

There are opportunities for all soldiers to earn college credit, even without attending class. Soldiers working on graveyard or rotating shifts, deploying overseas or to the field, or going on extended temporary duty can earn college credit. Many soldiers have mistakenly come to believe that college credit can be obtained only by sitting in a classroom during daytime hours as a professor lectures. Most soldiers are unaware of the many nontraditional programs and opportunities.

There are several ways in which soldiers can get college credits: for military education and training; by examination in subjects for which they can get complete advance study materials; through accredited colleges that have nontraditional education programs designed especially for military personnel; from Servicemembers Opportunity Colleges (SOC)—an extensive network of colleges that have coordinated programs among themselves, which are designed to accommodate a servicemember by minimizing residency requirements and maximizing the ability to transfer credits between schools; and from the Defense Activity for Non-Traditional Educational Support (DANTES), a distance learning program established to serve military personnel and their particular needs. These programs are for the soldier who wants to gain college credit and an associate's or bachelor's degree. They are called nontraditional because they provide ambitious soldiers with unique opportunities to acquire a college education.

The purpose of this guide is to make the quest for a college education easier by informing soldiers of and guiding them in the many nontraditional opportunities there are to pursue a college education while on active duty.

PART I

PLANNING
FOR SUCCESS

1

Establish Educational Goals

"How do I begin?" you may ask. Your journey has already begun. Your interest in earning college credit indicates that you have the desire to improve yourself and your position in life. Reading this book demonstrates that you have the willingness to act and take the necessary positive steps toward that better life. So, you ask, what are these steps? The educational journey has been broken down into five steps:

Step 1: Establish your educational goals.
Step 2: Develop an educational plan of attack.
Step 3: Begin your educational attack.
Step 4: Monitor your success and remain persistent.
Step 5: Accomplish your goals, set them higher, and start again.

The first step is covered in this chapter, and the other steps are covered in the following two chapters. Using these steps will not help you work harder, but they will help you work smarter. By following them, you can accomplish any level of college education you desire.

HOW DO YOU ESTABLISH AN EDUCATIONAL GOAL?

Establishing a goal should always be the first step in any endeavor. Before you begin a task, you must know the objective or goal of that task. When you take your Army Physical Fitness Test (APFT), you establish a goal for yourself before the test begins. Your goal on the APFT may be to score at least 270 points, or your goal may be to max the APFT. Either way, you establish a goal for yourself. The same should be true with your education.

So, what is your educational goal? For many soldiers, determining their goals may be the toughest part. Everyone agrees that it is easier to monitor your progress once you have a direction in life and know where

you are going. Many soldiers can develop their educational goals by
closely examining their career goals. Ask yourself where you want to be
in your career five, ten, or fifteen years from now. By developing a clear
career goal, you can easily determine a complementary educational goal.
In this way, soldiers focus on a practical application of their time and efforts that results in tangible benefits. Following are four real-life examples
of complementary career and educational goals.

Example One: Specialist Roberts wants to be promoted to Sergeant.
Although she has not yet appeared before the promotion board, she is
thinking ahead. She has already earned 16 promotion points toward civilian education. She determines that if she can max the civilian education
section of her promotion point worksheet, she will be 100 points ahead of
most of her peers who have not yet considered college. She also decides
that the 100 points would serve as a clear indication of her desire for self-
improvement when she appears before the promotion board. Specialist
Roberts knows that each semester hour of college equals 1 promotion
point in the civilian education section of the promotion point worksheet. If
she already has 16 points and needs 84 more points to max her civilian education, she must complete 84 semester hours of college.

Her short-term career goal: Earn promotion to Sergeant.

Her educational goal: Complete 84 semester hours of college.

Example Two: Sergeant First Class Hogan thinks that he deserves to
be promoted to Master Sergeant. He has been in the Army for sixteen
years, and during that time he has served as a drill instructor and a platoon
sergeant, was deployed to Saudi Arabia during the Gulf War, has scored
above 290 points on nearly every APFT, and has consistently been given
excellent ratings by all his supervisors. The only problem is that there are
few promotions to Master Sergeant in his career field, and promotions
within his Military Occupational Specialty (MOS) are very competitive.
Sergeant Hogan knows that his only weakness is in civilian education.
Additionally, Sergeant Hogan has been speaking with Army Career and
Alumni Program (ACAP) counselors about his prospects for civilian employment after retirement. The counselors at ACAP have strongly advised
him to obtain as much college as possible before retirement. Sergeant
Hogan decides that an associate in arts (AA) degree will both prepare him
for life after the military and substantially increase his chances for promotion to Master Sergeant. He decides to seek and complete his AA degree
during his last four years of military service.

His career goals: Earn promotion to Master Sergeant and prepare for
retirement.

His educational goal: Earn his AA degree.

Example Three: Sergeant Paty plans to apply to Officer Candidate School (OCS). He has already taken some college classes and now has 90 quarter hours of college. He knows that in order to apply, he must have, among other things, a minimum of 60 semester hours or 90 quarter hours of college. Although he meets the minimum college requirements, Sergeant Paty is aware that few applicants are selected for OCS without a bachelor's degree, which generally requires 180 quarter hours or 120 semester hours. After speaking with his company commander about a recommendation for OCS, Sergeant Paty decides to pursue the quickest route to completing a bachelor's degree.

His career goal: Attend OCS and become an officer.

His educational goal: Earn his bachelor's degree.

Example Four: Specialist Langert has just been promoted from Private First Class. She is happy about the promotion, and although she enjoys her job, her real desire is to become a high school physical education teacher. She joined the Army only to get money for college. Her plan was to save as much money as possible during her four-year stint, then get out of the Army and use the GI Bill and her savings to attend college full-time. Specialist Langert's savings are not as much as she would like them to be, and she has just read about budget cutbacks in public education in her home state. To her surprise, her Education Services Officer (ESO) has just told her about the Troops to Teachers Program and how she can get a teaching job lined up before she leaves the military. Based on the advice of her ESO, Specialist Langert decides that she should earn her bachelor's degree before she separates from the Army if she is to have a serious chance of pursuing her dream of becoming a teacher.

Her career goal: Become a high school teacher.

Her educational goal: Earn her bachelor's degree.

HOW DO YOU GET HELP IN DETERMINING YOUR EDUCATIONAL GOAL?

If you are still undecided about your career or educational goals, perhaps you need professional one-on-one guidance. Your ESO can help you make your career decision with valuable career advice and counseling. Your ESO can also administer a variety of tests that measure your interest and aptitude in different fields. These tests can help point you in a direction to determine your goal. Two of these interest and aptitude tests are described below.

Career Assessment Inventory
The Career Assessment Inventory (CAI) is an objective vocational interest test that compares occupational interests and personality preferences with those of individuals in over 100 specific careers. There is also an enhanced version of the CAI that focuses on careers requiring a secondary education. ESOs and guidance counselors use the CAI to assist those who need career guidance and adult career development. The CAI helps soldiers focus on interests that are important to them in making educational and occupational choices. It also assists in identifying a career direction and selecting major areas of study, advising individuals who are reentering the workforce or considering a career change, screening job applicants, and providing career development assistance.

Career Planning Program
The Career Planning Program (CPP) is a guidance-oriented system designed to help individuals identify and explore relevant occupations and educational programs. This test consists of an ability test battery, an interest inventory, scales for assessing career-related experiences, and a background and plans inventory. The CPP normally takes about two and a half hours and is well worth the time. The test helps counselors measure a person's interests, experience, and abilities. The CPP also uses a group guidance technique that allows the counselor to assist more people with career and educational planning. This technique is mutually beneficial, because it teaches individuals how to gather and consider information that is vital to their own career and educational planning processes. The counselors help individuals help themselves.

Keep a Diary or Journal
When considering what your goals should be, it is a good idea to keep a small notebook or diary of your ideas. Carry the notebook with you everywhere, and immediately write down any ideas that come to mind. It is also a good idea to place the notebook and a pen beside your bed at night. Think about your goals before going to sleep. Many people find that they are full of fresh ideas or struck by an inspiration upon awakening. Immediately write down any new ideas, before they are forgotten. After you have decided on your career and educational goals, note them in

the notebook. You may also want to follow the advice of Dan O'Brien, the 1996 Olympic decathlon gold medalist. He recommends that you write your goals down and carry them in your pocket. With your goals always in your mind, in your notebook, or in your pocket, you will never lose sight of the purpose of your work. Now it is time to move on to step two.

2

Develop a Plan of Attack

Okay, so you have developed your goals and have written them down in your notebook. You know where you are now and where you want to be. You have determined how a college education can help get you there. Now you have to tackle step two and develop your educational plan of attack. It is important not to underestimate the need for a plan. The Army now requires a degree plan from soldiers who desire tuition assistance. This requirement, which goes into effect after a soldier has completed three tuition assistance-funded classes, is now being strictly enforced.

To make it easier, this step is broken down into four smaller steps:

Keep your plan a secret.

Research and assess your available educational opportunities.

Do the math and determine exactly what you need.

Make a goal schedule and put it in writing.

KEEP YOUR PLAN A SECRET

Maintaining a positive attitude is extremely important to accomplishing any goal. It is true that most people are their own worst critics and one critic is usually enough. Unless naysayers inspire you to work harder or you have an exceptionally high level of confidence, it is best to keep your plan a secret. Many people, even friends, will unintentionally drain your confidence with their doubts and negative comments. The higher or more ambitious your goal, the more you are at risk. It makes people feel better to think that if they cannot do something, no one can. The truth is that many people feel threatened by those who try to improve themselves. Because your positive attitude is so important to success, share your intimate ideas and plans only with those you trust to be positive and support you.

RESEARCH AND ASSESS
YOUR AVAILABLE EDUCATIONAL OPPORTUNITIES

When seeking information about your college credit opportunities, there is no substitute for firsthand knowledge, but there are shortcuts. The chapters of this book detailing nontraditional educational resources are one of those shortcuts. These chapters contain firsthand knowledge gained from years of experience and research. Other sources of valuable information are the professionals at your local education center. These professionals can offer information, counseling, and advice on many of the resources covered in this book. Take advantage of their services, but read the chapters on nontraditional educational resources first. These chapters will save you time, help you ask more intelligent questions, and help you zero in on those opportunities best suited to your particular situation and goals.

DO THE MATH AND DETERMINE
EXACTLY WHAT YOU NEED

Dissect your goal and determine exactly what you need to accomplish it. Do you need to earn 50 more semester hours of college to max the civilian education section of the promotion point worksheet? Do you need 100 semester hours in specific courses to complete a bachelor's degree? Using this book, the resources at your Army Education Center (AEC), and advice from your ESO, determine the component parts of your educational goal and exactly what you need to accomplish that goal. Break your goal down to the point where you know exactly which college classes and how much credit you need to earn the degree you want or the number of semester hours needed for promotion.

MAKE A GOAL SCHEDULE AND PUT IT IN WRITING

You know exactly what your educational goal is, you know what opportunities exist to pursue that goal, and you have dissected and measured exactly what you need to do to accomplish your goal. Now it is time to develop a schedule for pursuing that goal (see the accompanying sample). A successful schedule is a catalyst to accomplishing any goal, but even more so with an educational goal. The most important parts of the schedule are the desired completion dates of your goal components. Write down a specific date by which you intend to accomplish each component of your

EDUCATION GOAL SCHEDULE FOR
SPECIALIST SUSANNE ROBERTS

January 1999–December 1999
1-year career goal: promotion to Sergeant
5-year career goal: undecided (but considering staying in the military)
1-year educational goal: complete 90 semester hours of college by
December 1999
5-year educational goal: undecided (considering a bachelor's degree)

**Progress toward goal
of 90 semester hours**

Milestones already accomplished:

Apr. 98:	Completed 2 classes worth 6 semester hours	6
July 98:	Signed SOCAD-2 agreement with Saint Leo College	
Aug. 98:	AARTS transcript sent to Saint Leo College	
Nov. 98:	Military experience (MOS and PLDC) evaluation complete	12

Projected milestones:

Jan.:	Take the General Mathematics CLEP Exam	6
	Enroll in 2 DANTES Distance Learning classes by correspondence	
Feb.:	3 week deployment to the field (study for upcoming exams)	
Mar.:	Take General English CLEP Exam (with essay)	6
	Take Intro to Philosophy course at Saint Leo (8-week term)	3
	Receive DANTES Distance Learning classes ordered in January	
Apr.:	Take Fundamentals of Counseling DSST	3
May:	Take General Science CLEP Exam	6
June:	Rotate to North Camp MFO, Egypt, for 30-day temporary duty	
	Take American History I CLEP Subject Exam at North Camp educ. center	3
	Take American Dream (Part I) ACT-PEP at North Camp educ. center	6

July:	Take General Social Sciences CLEP Exam	6
Aug.:	Take Criminal Justice DSST	3
Sept.:	Complete both Distance Learning courses received in April	6
	Order two more Distance Learning courses	
Oct.:	Take Sociology GRE	3–30
Nov.:	Take Spanish Level 1 and 2 CLEP Subject Exam	6
Dec.:	Holiday staff duty Dec. 1–7 (view Annenberg tapes and study)	
	Leave Dec. 15–31 (relax and make plan for next year)	

Total progress
toward goal
75–102 semester hours

---

goal. For example, write down the date you intend to take an examination for college credit or the date you intend to complete a college correspondence course. Make the dates as practical as possible, but do not worry, they can be fine-tuned later. Post these dates, the components of your goal, and the entire goal itself in a private but noticeable place in your home or room. The refrigerator, the inside of a wall locker, your notebook, or any personal area that you see daily are all good places to post these items.

3

Begin Your Attack
and Monitor Your Success

By now you should have everything you need to begin your attack. You have developed a goal, you know your available resources, you have created a plan to pursue your goal, and you have made a schedule to accomplish each component part of your goal by a specific date. The only thing left to do is to get started.

BE PREPARED
Being prepared is more than a motto for the Boy Scouts; it is also one of the many secrets of success. If you have made it to this point, you already know what it means to be prepared. Part of being prepared is having a clear vision or a goal; studying and researching the problem, the obstacle, and the goal; establishing a clear path or plan to success; and implementing a schedule. In short, you are already prepared.

BE OPTIMISTIC
General Colin Powell once remarked that "perpetual optimism is a force multiplier." The spirit of optimism has been the most important factor in countless battles throughout human history, and your battle is no different. If you lose your can-do attitude, you have lost the battle.

BE DISCIPLINED
Remember, no one can do it for you. You have to be committed to sticking to your schedule. If your schedule dictates that you study two hours each day in preparation for a college correspondence course, you must study two hours. Put your schedule ahead of all other unnecessary activities. If you are serious, studying will take first priority over entertainment, television, and beer with your buddies. Everyone has heard that if you

want something badly enough, you should be willing to work for it. If this is not true of your educational goals, then you probably do not want them badly enough. At the same time, do not overdo it. If you tend to be a workaholic, remember to take breaks and enjoy life. The idea is to be disciplined enough to work as hard as necessary to accomplish your goal without inducing burnout.

MONITOR YOUR SUCCESS
It is important to monitor the success, or lack thereof, of all your efforts. Again, optimism is extremely important, but it may be unrealistic to expect to accomplish everything you strive for on the first try. You must be prepared to modify your plan and your schedule based on your positive and negative experiences. If you are ahead of schedule, then perhaps you have room for a more ambitious goal. If you are behind schedule, then perhaps you were overly optimistic. Review your efforts at least once a week and make notes about both your successes and your failures in the personal goals notebook mentioned earlier. Continually monitoring your efforts is important to success, as it allows you to maximize lessons learned from both success and failure.

REMAIN PERSISTENT
Yes, failure as well as success is part of the process of pursuing your goal. The objective is to remain persistent and optimistic and to realize that often more is gained from failure than from success. When you broke your educational goal down into component parts, you were reducing your goal to the lowest denominator. The lowest denominator is important, because it represents the small steps toward your goal. Remain persistent and do something every day, even if it takes only five minutes, to push onward toward your educational goal. By remaining persistent, you will notice that your small steps add up quickly, and before you know it, you will have traveled miles toward your goal.

ACCOMPLISH YOUR GOALS
By following the steps outlined in the previous pages, using the information in this book, and following the advice of the professional counselors at your AEC, you can accomplish your educational goals. The only step left will be to set your goals higher and start again.

PART II

THE RESOURCES TO MAKE IT HAPPEN

4

Educational Opportunities and Resources

The opportunities available to soldiers who want to pursue a college education while on active duty are almost limitless. Many soldiers, however, believe that on-campus daytime courses taught at a local college are the only option. Although this is the most common traditional way to obtain college credit, it is only one of many. In fact, there are hundreds of nontraditional sources and opportunities available for soldiers who want to earn college credit.

WHAT IS THE DIFFERENCE BETWEEN TRADITIONAL AND NONTRADITIONAL EDUCATIONAL OPPORTUNITIES?
Traditional educational opportunities consist of on-campus daytime courses taught at a postsecondary institution such as a local college or university. According to the U.S. Department of Education, National Center for Education Statistics, there are nearly 10,000 such postsecondary schools in the United States. These colleges and universities cater mostly to a young student body. Their programs are rigid, with institutionally structured rules and regulations designed for less mature men and women. These students normally attend school as full-time students and usually have no other responsibilities. Many of these colleges and universities offer classes that are available only during the daytime to full-time students.

Nontraditional educational opportunities are those that break with the traditional concept that all learning must occur at a young age, in a daytime classroom setting. These opportunities include, but are not limited to, evening classes, weekend classes, summer classes, independent study, correspondence courses, classes taught over the Internet, video classes, telecourses, contract learning, college credit by examination, and college credit for life experience. This book was specifically written to promote the educational opportunities available through nontraditional methods.

WHICH IS BETTER, TRADITIONAL OR NONTRADITIONAL EDUCATION?

You will have to decide which route is best for you. If you are a soldier on active duty, however, your opportunities to pursue college traditionally are often limited by the nature of your military duties. When most soldiers complain that they cannot pursue college credit, they are referring to college credit obtained by traditional methods. Most soldiers are simply unaware that there are many nontraditional ways to pursue the same college education they could obtain using the traditional route. Nontraditional methods are also easier, cheaper, less utilized, and less publicized.

NONTRADITIONAL EDUCATIONAL RESOURCES

Nontraditional educational opportunities are those that break with the traditional concepts of college learning. Listed below are some of the largest, easiest to use, and cheapest resources of nontraditional college credit available to soldiers today. Each resource listed is covered in detail in subsequent chapters:

AARTS Transcript—college credit for military experience

DD Form 295—college credit for military experience

ACT-PEP: Regents College Examinations—college credit by examination

CLEP Tests—college credit by examination

DANTES Examinations—college credit by examination

Annenberg Program—video preparation for college credit examinations

GRE Tests—undergraduate curricula achievement/graduate school entrance examinations used by selected institutions to award college credit

DANTES Distance Learning Program—college credit for courses offered through the mail, on video, or over the computer

Regents College—nontraditional college with unique degree completion programs

Thomas Edison State College—nontraditional college with unique degree completion programs

SOC—contract learning for military personnel with unique degree completion programs

Army Education Center and other resources—miscellaneous programs and information on many other nontraditional programs

**Can Army Reserve and National Guard Personnel
Use These Nontraditional Programs?**
Both Army Reserve and Army National Guard personnel are eligible to use all the programs mentioned above. The only partial exception is the AARTS Program. Only active military service performed and schools attended while on active duty will be noted on the AARTS transcript.

5

College Credit
for Military Experience

The Army/American Council on Education (ACE) Registry Transcript System (AARTS) compiles a transcript that is an official record of your military education and is used to translate your military experience into college credit. It lists most of your active-duty military training courses and educational experiences in a format similar to that of transcripts from high school or college. In addition, the AARTS transcript includes the ACE college credit recommendations for each of the military courses and experiences listed.

WHAT IS THE PURPOSE OF THE AARTS TRANSCRIPT?

The purpose of the AARTS transcript is to facilitate the awarding of college credit to soldiers for their completed military courses and training. Most colleges and universities award college credit for military training in accordance with the recommendations in the *Guide to the Evaluation of Educational Experiences in the Armed Services,* published by ACE. The Army and ACE cooperate to maintain the AARTS. A transcript from AARTS saves college officials time, ensures the accuracy of ACE recommendations, and allows colleges to award credit more easily to soldiers for their training and experience.

WHAT INFORMATION IS INCLUDED
ON THE AARTS TRANSCRIPT?

The AARTS transcript includes important information about a soldier's military career and experiences. The transcript is divided into the following sections:

Biographical Data: The soldier's name, social security number, rank, military status, time in service, and highest academic level completed.

Test Scores: CLEP, ACT-PEP, SAT, and DANTES DSST scores; test dates; test numbers; test titles; and the ACE recommended college credit for each test taken through DANTES or a military education center.

Military Course Descriptions: Entries for Basic Training and Advanced Individual Training (AIT) courses completed; completed Noncommissioned Officer Education System (NCOES) courses, such as Primary Leadership Development Course (PLDC), Basic NCO Course (BNCOC), and Advanced NCO Course (ANCOC); other completed formal service school courses that were longer than forty-five hours; course titles; course locations; dates of attendance; course descriptions; Army and ACE course identification numbers; and the ACE recommended college credit for each course.

Military Experience: All primary, secondary, and duty Military Occupational Specialties (MOSs) held by the soldier; duty descriptions for all MOSs performed; and the ACE recommended college credit.

Other Learning Experiences: Data on any completed courses that are pending evaluation by ACE, completed courses with information not yet available in the computer system, or completed courses that ACE is not able to evaluate.

WHAT INFORMATION IS NOT INCLUDED ON THE AARTS TRANSCRIPT?

Currently, the AARTS transcript does not include information on correspondence courses; local command training courses; headstart courses; training or experience for reserve components; or training, courses, or experience in other branches of the military, other government agencies, or civilian organizations.

HOW CAN YOU GET A TRANSCRIPT OF COURSES NOT LISTED ON THE AARTS TRANSCRIPT?

Military courses not included on the AARTS transcript can be documented using DD Form 295, which is covered later in this chapter. A transcript of military courses taught or offered through the Air Force may be requested from the Community College of the Air Force, which is covered in Chapter 11. Most government and civilian agencies also provide transcripts of any courses completed with their organizations. Before writing to request a transcript, however, it is a good idea to call and verify the cost and proper mailing address. Even some government agencies charge transcript fees.

**ARMY/AMERICAN COUNCIL ON EDUCATION
REGISTRY TRANSCRIPT**

```
06/16/97              ** PERSONAL COPY **                 PAGE 1

   TRANSCRIPT SENT TO:                NAME: DOE JOHN DAVID
                                      SSN:  123-45-6789
                                      RANK: SPECIALIST
   SPC JOHN DOE                       MILITARY STATUS:  ACTIVE
   9876 MAIN STREET                   TIME IN SERVICE:
   WASHINGTON, DC  20340                 3 YEARS, 5 MONTHS
                                      ACADEMIC LEVEL COMPLETED:
                                         2-YEAR COLLEGE
   AARTS ID: 97-12345
   ----------------------- MILITARY COURSE COMPLETIONS ---------------------

   COURSE: BASIC TRAINING                   ACE GUIDE ID NUMBER:
           (RECRUIT TRAINING)                   AR-2201-0399

   DESCRIPTION: UPON COMPLETION OF THIS PROGRAM OF INSTRUCTION, THE GRADUATED
   RECRUIT WILL BE ABLE TO DEMONSTRATE: 1) GENERAL KNOWLEDGE OF MILITARY
   ORGANIZATION AND CULTURE; 2) MASTERY OF INDIVIDUAL AND GROUP COMBAT SKILLS
   INCLUDING MARKSMANSHIP AND FIRST AID; 3) ACHIEVEMENT OF MINIMAL PHYSICAL
   CONDITIONING STANDARDS; AND 4) ABILITY TO SUCCESSFULLY APPLY BASIC SAFETY
   AND LIVING SKILLS IN THE OUTDOOR ENVIRONMENT.  INSTRUCTION INCLUDES
   LECTURES, DEMONSTRATIONS, AND PERFORMANCE EXERCISES IN BASIC MILITARY
   CULTURE/SUBJECTS INCLUDING MARKSMANSHIP, PHYSICAL CONDITIONING, FIRST AID
   AND OUTDOOR ADAPTATION/LIVING SKILLS.

   ACE CREDIT RECOMMENDATION:  IN THE LOWER-DIVISION BACCALAUREATE/ASSOCIATE
   DEGREE CATEGORY, 1 SEMESTER HOUR IN PERSONAL PHYSICAL CONDITIONING, 1 IN
   OUTDOOR SKILLS PRACTICUM, 1 IN MARKSMANSHIP, AND 1 IN FIRST AID.

                        ----------------------------

   COURSE: PRIMARY LEADERSHIP DEVELOPMENT     ACE GUIDE ID NUMBER:
           NCO ACADEMY                            AR-2201-0253
           FT. STEWART, GA

   DATES TAKEN: 11/21/96-12/20/96  ARMY COURSE NUMBER:  698-04-PLDC

   DESCRIPTION: UPON COMPLETION OF THE COURSE, THE STUDENT WILL BE ABLE TO
   PERFORM ALL BASIC TASKS RELATING TO THE NONCOMMISSIONED OFFICER LEADERSHIP
   RESPONSIBILITY.  LECTURES AND PRACTICAL EXERCISES IN LEADERSHIP,
   COMMUNICATIONS, RESOURCE MANAGEMENT, TRAINING MANAGEMENT, AND PROFESSIONAL
   SKILLS, INCLUDING INTRODUCTION TO LEADERSHIP, PRINCIPLES OF LEADERSHIP,
   HUMAN BEHAVIOR, CHARACTER OF LEADERS, ETHICS, PROBLEM SOLVING, LEADERSHIP
   STYLES, PRINCIPLES OF MOTIVATION, COUNSELING, AND RESPONSIBILITY OF
   AUTHORITY.  EMPHASIS IS ON TEACHING TO TEACH AND TO LEAD SOLDIERS WHO WILL
   ************************** CONTINUED ON PAGE 2 **************************
```

**ARMY/AMERICAN COUNCIL ON EDUCATION
REGISTRY TRANSCRIPT**

06/16/97   ** PERSONAL COPY **   PAGE 2

TRANSCRIPT SENT TO: NAME: DOE JOHN DAVID
SPC JOHN DOE   SSN: 123-45-6789
9876 MAIN STREET
WASHINGTON, DC 20340

----------------------- MILITARY COURSE COMPLETIONS ---------------------
WORK AND FIGHT UNDER THEIR LEADERSHIP. COURSE CONTENT INCLUDES
DEFENSIVE/OFFENSIVE OPERATIONS, AND FIELD TRAINING EXERCISES IN WHICH
PREVIOUS LESSONS ARE APPLIED.

ACE CREDIT RECOMMENDATION: IN THE LOWER-DIVISION BACCALAUREATE/ASSOCIATE
DEGREE CATEGORY, 1 SEMESTER HOUR IN PRINCIPLES OF SUPERVISION, 2 IN
MILITARY SCIENCE (12/91).

------------------------------ TEST SCORES ------------------------------
DANTES SUBJECT STANDARDIZED TESTS (DSST)

    -    SE470   GEOGRAPHY
DATE: 05/18/94   SCORE: 064 ACE RECOMMENDED PASSING SCORE: 046
                                ACE RECOMMENDED CREDIT: 03 SH

COLLEGE LEVEL EXAMINATION PROGRAM (CLEP) - GENERAL

    -    03191   MATHEMATICS
DATE: 05/11/94   SCORE: 626 MS: 63   MC: 63
ACE RECOMMENDED PASSING SCORE: 421   ACE RECOMMENDED CREDIT: 06 SH

-------------------------- MILITARY EXPERIENCE ------------------------
MILITARY OCCUPATIONAL SPECIALTIES HELD: 98C10 PRIMARY   (07/94-06/97)
                                         98C10 DUTY

MILITARY OCCUPATIONAL SPECIALTY GROUP: 98C   ACE GUIDE ID NUMBER:
TITLE: SIGNALS INTELLIGENCE ANALYST   MOS 98C-003
        (SIGINT ANALYST)
DESCRIPTION OF 98C10: GATHERS, SORTS, AND SCANS INTERCEPTED MESSAGES AND
SIGNALS, AND PERFORMS INITIAL ANALYSIS TO ESTABLISH COMMUNICATIONS
PATTERNS; ISOLATES VALID MESSAGE TRAFFIC; REDUCES COMMUNICATIONS DATA INTO
AUTOMATIC DATA PROCESSING FORMAT; OPERATES COMMUNICATIONS EQUIPMENT FOR
************************* CONTINUED ON PAGE 3 *************************

**ARMY/AMERICAN COUNCIL ON EDUCATION
REGISTRY TRANSCRIPT**

06/16/97   ** PERSONAL COPY **   PAGE 3

TRANSCRIPT SENT TO: NAME: DOE JOHN DAVID
SPC JOHN DOE   SSN: 123-45-6789
9876 MAIN STREET
WASHINGTON, DC 20340

--------------------------- MILITARY EXPERIENCE -------------------------

REPORTING AND COORDINATION; TYPES AT A MINIMUM RATE OF 24 WORDS PER MINUTE;
HAS KNOWLEDGE OF THE GEOGRAPHY AND CULTURE OF THE AREA FROM WHICH
INTERCEPTED COMMUNICATIONS ORIGINATE; MAY ACQUIRE A TECHNICAL VOCABULARY IN
ONE OR MORE FOREIGN LANGUAGE(S).

ACE CREDIT RECOMMENDATION FOR 98C10: IN THE VOCATIONAL CERTIFICATE
CATEGORY, 3 SEMESTER HOURS IN ELECTRONIC SYSTEMS OPERATIONS. IN THE LOWER-
DIVISION BACCALAUREATE/ASSOCIATE DEGREE CATEGORY, 3 SEMESTER HOURS IN
WRITTEN COMMUNICATIONS, 3 IN KEYBOARDING, 1 IN COMPUTER LITERACY, AND 2 IN
GEOGRAPHY, AND CREDIT FOR FOREIGN LANGUAGE PROFICIENCY ON THE BASIS OF
INSTITUTIONAL EVALUATION (9/88).

----------------------- OTHER LEARNING EXPERIENCES ----------------------

    COURSE NUMBER/   COURSE TITLE/
    DATES TAKEN   COURSE LOCATION

    -------------------   -------------------

    X3AB420230-001 (98C10)   EW/CRYPTOLOGIC TRAFFIC ANALYST
    03/20/94-/07/14/94   USAF TECHNICAL TRAINING SCHOOL
                                      GOODFELLOW AFB, TX

    ************* LAST ENTRY ********** PAGE 3 OF 3 ********************

HOW MUCH DOES AN AARTS TRANSCRIPT COST?
The AARTS transcript is free.

HOW DO YOU GET A COPY OF THE AARTS TRANSCRIPT?
To obtain a copy of your AARTS transcript, pick up DA Form 5454-R, Request for Army/American Council on Education Registry Transcript, from your education center and mail it to AARTS Operations Center, Fort Leavenworth, KS 66027-5073. You can also send the request via fax to the AARTS fax number: (913) 684-2011. If you cannot obtain DA Form 5454-R, simply write a letter requesting your AARTS transcript and send it to the same address or fax number above. Be sure that all requests include your full name, social security number, basic active service date, and the address or addresses where you would like AARTS to send your transcript. If you do not already have a copy of your own AARTS transcript, you should request one immediately.

WHY DO YOU NEED TO KEEP A COPY OF YOUR AARTS TRANSCRIPT?
No ambitious NCO or soldier ever allows his or her records to appear before a promotion or selection board without first reviewing them to ensure that they are 100 percent accurate and up-to-date. The same should be true of your educational records. The people at AARTS do an excellent job, but mistakes are made occasionally. Additionally, it may take AARTS up to three months to update your records after promotion, course completions, and other changes. Regardless of the reason, the earlier a mistake is discovered, the easier it is to correct.

HOW DO YOU MAKE CORRECTIONS TO YOU AARTS TRANSCRIPT?
If you discover errors in your AARTS transcript, write a letter detailing the errors and mail it to AARTS Operations Center, Fort Leavenworth, KS 66027-5073. As with the request for your AARTS transcript, this letter should include your full name, social security number, basic active service date, and the address or addresses where you would like AARTS to send the corrected transcript. Be sure to include with your letter certified copies of documents that refute the errors. A certified copy of your DA Form 2A, DA Form 2-1, DA Form 1059, or course completion certificate will generally suffice to correct most errors.

CAN THE AARTS TRANSCRIPT BE USED
AS A RÉSUMÉ OF MILITARY EXPERIENCE?

The AARTS transcript can be a valuable supplement or attachment to the résumé of a retiring or separating soldier, but the transcript itself is not a résumé. Because the AARTS transcript includes military experiences and job descriptions, it can be an important tool for those seeking to provide potential employers with a complete understanding of their military skills and responsibilities.

IS THERE ANYONE WHO CANNOT USE AARTS
TO REQUEST A TRANSCRIPT?

Only enlisted Army personnel and veterans can use AARTS to request a transcript. Members of the Army Reserve, warrant officers, commissioned officers, and members of other services cannot receive AARTS transcripts. Additionally, soldiers are ineligible to receive AARTS transcripts if they have a basic active service date of September 30, 1981, or earlier. If you are ineligible to use AARTS, you can still use DD Form 295 to request evaluation of your military training and experience.

WHAT IS DD FORM 295?

DD Form 295 is officially known as the Application for the Evaluation of Learning Experiences During Military Service. DD Form 295 was used extensively by soldiers to receive credit for their military experiences and training before AARTS was implemented. Due to the fact that not all soldiers are eligible to use AARTS, DD Form 295 remains in service.

HOW DO YOU USE DD FORM 295 INSTEAD OF AARTS?

The form is available at most military education centers or local Military Personnel Offices (MILPOs). Complete the form with the assistance of your ESO, taking great care to ensure that all data are entered correctly. Complete sections 1 through 15. The information you provide, such as rank, address, and courses completed, is essentially the same as that found on the AARTS transcript. Your ESO or MILPO official should complete all information required in sections 16 through 18. Do not use abbreviations to describe your official training or courses, because certifying officials may not know the meaning of unfamiliar acronyms or abbreviations. After you complete the form, sign it and take it to your certifying officer, usually a MILPO official. The certifying official verifies the accuracy of the data entered on the DD Form 295 using your personnel records. If your personnel records are inaccurate, your DD Form 295 will likely be

APPLICATION FOR THE EVALUATION OF
LEARNING EXPERIENCES DURING MILITARY SERVICE

_____
(Date)

TO: (Name and address of educational
institution, agency, or employer)

EVALUATION REQUEST FOR:

_____
(Name of Applicant)

_____
(Social Security Number)

ATTENTION:

Dear Official:

The applicant named above has requested that the attached summary of educational achievements, accomplished while in the Armed Forces of the United States, be forwarded to you for review and evaluation.

The American Council on Education publishes the *Guide to the Evaluation of Educational Experiences in the Armed Services* which includes postsecondary credit evaluations of military learning experiences. The 1954 edition of the *Guide* contains recommendations for formal courses offered by the Armed Services during the period 1941 to 1954. The current edition contains credit recommendations for (1) military training courses offered after 1954; (2) Army military occupational specialties (MOS's) for enlisted personnel and warrant officers; (3) ratings held by Navy and Coast Guard enlisted personnel; and (4) occupational designators held by Navy and Coast Guard warrant officers and Navy limited duty officers. In addition to recommendations for semester hour credits, some Army enlisted MOS's and Navy ratings also have recommendations for advanced standing in apprentice training programs.

The American Council on Education maintains an advisory service to provide credit recommendations for courses and tests, MOS's, ratings, and other occupations evaluated after the publication date of the current *Guide*. Credit recommendations are provided to officials of schools, state departments of education or other educational institutions, employers, apprenticeship training directors, labor union and trade association officials, military education officers and applicants. *Credit recommendations are not provided to officials at the applicant's request.* Authorized persons may write directly to the Military Evaluations Program Office, American Council on Education, One Dupont Circle, N.W., Washington, D.C. 20036-1193.

The evaluation of this applicant's learning experiences, as well as any guidance which you may provide, should be sent directly to the applicant at the address shown in block 6 on page 3. Your interest is genuinely appreciated.

Sincerely,

_____
(Education Officer)

DD Form 295, NOV 86   Previous editions are obsolete.   Page 1 of 4 Pages
1207/330

Privacy Act Statement

AUTHORITY: 5 USC 301 and EO 9397, November 1943 (SSN).

PRINCIPAL PURPOSE: To permit authorized agencies to evaluate military experience for academic placement and/or employment.

ROUTINE USES: Used at the request of the individual for the evaluation of military training.

DISCLOSURE: Voluntary; however, failure to provide requested information impedes the evaluation process by educational institutions or potential employers.

INSTRUCTIONS TO APPLICANT

DD Form 295 is for your convenience in applying for evaluation of your educational experiences during military service. Give as much detailed information as possible. Include additional information on separate sheets, if necessary.

You are encouraged to write a preliminary letter to the school or agency concerned, explaining your interest in its evaluation of your records for the continuance of your education. Training, correspondence study, or special experiences not described on this form, which you believe would be of interest to those reviewing your case, should be included in this letter.

The applicant should:

a. Complete items 1 through 15.

b. If you have attended college or completed any college correspondence courses, ask that college to send a transcript to the Registrar of the evaluating agency that this form is addressed to. DO NOT LIST ANY COLLEGE OR UNIVERSITY COURSES ON THIS FORM.

c. If you have completed any college-level standardized examinations for credit, such as USAFI or DANTES Subject Standardized Tests, or CLEP, ask the appropriate agency to send a score report to the Registrar of the evaluating agency that this form is addressed to. DO NOT LIST ANY EXAMINATIONS ON THIS FORM.

d. After completion, submit this DD Form 295 to the Certifying Officer.

INSTRUCTIONS TO CERTIFYING OFFICER
(Custodian of Personnel Records)

DD Form 295 is intended to provide factual information that schools and other evaluating agencies require for evaluation of the applicant's educational achievement. CERTIFYING OFFICERS WILL NOT MAKE RECOMMENDATIONS REGARDING CREDIT TO BE AWARDED.

The certifying officer should:

a. Complete items 16 through 18.

b. Insure that the information provided in Section II is documented in the applicant's Service Record. Names of schools or courses should not be abbreviated.

c. Send this DD Form 295 to the Education Officer.

INSTRUCTIONS TO EDUCATION OFFICER

The education officer should:

a. Complete item 19.

b. Counsel the service member.

c. Complete page 1. The name and address of the evaluating agency should be the same as that listed at the top of page 3 of this form.

PAGE 1 IS IN ADDITION TO, AND NOT A SUBSTITUTE FOR, THE LETTER TO BE WRITTEN TO THE EVALUATING AGENCY BY THE APPLICANT.

d. Mail DD Form 295 directly to the designated evaluating agency.

DD Form 295, NOV 86   Page 2 of 4 Pages

APPLICATION FOR THE EVALUATION OF LEARNING EXPERIENCES
DURING MILITARY SERVICE

TO (Name and address of educational institution, agency, or employer)

SECTION I - TO BE COMPLETED BY APPLICANT

1. NAME (Last, First, Middle Initial)	2. GRADE/RANK OR RATING	3. SOCIAL SECURITY NO.	4. PREVIOUS SERVICE NUMBER(S)

5. PRESENT BRANCH OF SERVICE (Includes National Guard and Reserve components)
☐ a. ARMY ☐ b. NAVY ☐ c. AIR FORCE ☐ d. MARINE CORPS ☐ e. COAST GUARD

6. APPLICANT'S MAILING ADDRESS FOR REPLY FROM EDUCATIONAL INSTITUTION

7. DATE OF BIRTH	8. PERMANENT HOME ADDRESS

CIVILIAN EDUCATION

9. HIGHEST GRADE OF SCHOOL COMPLETED (X one)
☐ 6 ☐ 7 ☐ 8 ☐ 9 ☐ 10 ☐ 11 ☐ 12

10. HIGHEST YEAR OF COLLEGE COMPLETED (X one)
☐ a. NONE ☐ b. FRESHMAN ☐ c. SOPHOMORE ☐ d. JUNIOR ☐ e. SENIOR

11. COLLEGE DEGREE EARNED (X if applicable)
☐ a. ASSOCIATE ☐ b. BACHELOR

12. EDUCATIONAL INSTITUTION LAST ATTENDED

a. NAME	b. MAILING ADDRESS

13. USAFI COURSES COMPLETED IN SERVICE (Prior to 1974)
(The applicant should request a transcript for all courses to be forwarded directly to the evaluating agency.)

a. CATALOG NUMBER AND TITLE OF COURSE (If no courses were taken, print NONE)	b. METHOD OF STUDY (Correspondence, self-teaching, locally conducted classes, etc.)	c. LOCATION WHERE COMPLETED	d. DATE COURSE COMPLETED
(1)			
(2)			
(3)			
(4)			
(5)			
(6)			
(7)			
(8)			

14. MILITARY CORRESPONDENCE COURSE COMPLETED
(The applicant should attach a copy of the course completion letter or certificate.)

a. COURSE NAME (If no courses were taken, print NONE)	b. COURSE SPONSOR (AIPD, MCI, ECI, CGI)	c. DATE COURSE COMPLETED
(1)		
(2)		
(3)		
(4)		
(5)		
(6)		
(7)		
(8)		
(9)		

15. APPLICANT CERTIFICATION: I have read the Privacy Act Statement on Page 2.

a. SIGNATURE	b. DATE SIGNED

DD Form 295, NOV 86   Page 3 of 4 Pages

SECTION II - TO BE COMPLETED BY CERTIFYING OFFICER
(Read instructions on Page 2 before completing this page)

16. FORMAL SERVICE SCHOOLS ATTENDED (If longer than one week) (If none, print NONE)

a. COURSE TITLE	b. MILITARY COURSE NUMBER	c. NAME OF SCHOOL, CITY, STATE	d. DATE ENTERED	e. LENGTH¹ (in weeks)	f. DATE COMPLETED	g. FINAL MARK AND/OR CLASS STANDING²	19. ACE GUIDE COURSE OR OCCUPATION IDENTIFICATION NO. (To be filled out in Education Center)
(1)							
(2)							
(3)							
(4)							
(5)							
(6)							
(7)							
(8)							
(9)							
(10)							

17. MILITARY OCCUPATIONAL HISTORY

a. MILITARY SPEC. CODE (MOS, AFSC, Rate, etc.)³	b. MILITARY OCCUPATIONAL TITLE (Do Not Abbreviate)	c. DATES HELD From (Mo/yr) To (Mo/yr)	d. MOS/SQT SCORE (For Army Enlisted Personnel⁴)
(1)			
(2)			
(3)			

NOTES: ¹Print SP if course length was self paced ²If information is available, give grade received. If class standing is shown, give number in class, e.g., 10 in 241 ³List most recent skill levels or grade ⁴MOS/SQT Evaluation Score and Date of evaluation

THIS APPLICATION MUST BE SIGNED BY AN OFFICER OR A DULY AUTHORIZED NONCOMMISSIONED OFFICER.
I certify that the information contained herein has been compared with official records, and that this information is correct.

18. CERTIFYING OFFICER

a. NAME (Print or Type)	b. GRADE/RANK	c. MILITARY ADDRESS (Include ZIP Code)
d. SIGNATURE	e. DATE SIGNED	

DD Form 295, NOV 86   ☆U.S. GOVERNMENT PRINTING OFFICE: 1990—261—871/11309   Page 4 of 4 Pages

inaccurate or the certifying official will refuse to certify it. After the form is complete and verified, take it to your ESO for research and counseling. The ESO completes section 19 using the ACE *Guide to the Evaluation of Educational Experiences in the Armed Services.* If the ESO cannot locate the correct exhibit, section 19 is left blank. All identifiers (title, number, location, dates, and length) must match those in the ACE guide. The ESO then completes page 1 of the form, signs it and mails it to the college from which the soldier is requesting credit. The DD Form 295 should not be sent to ACE unless the courses are not found in the ACE guide. It is recommended that the soldier provide the college with a cover letter requesting its review of the DD Form 295. Most college officials usually grant credit to a soldier as long as it is appropriate and justifiable. It is a good idea to suggest that the DD Form 295 be forwarded to ACE if the school has any questions.

6

College Credit
by Examination

Examinations for college credit are nationally and internationally recognized testing programs that have been evaluated and approved by the American Council on Education (ACE) to grant college credit for experience, knowledge, and training obtained outside the traditional classroom setting. These examinations, which are listed on the following pages, represent the single greatest nontraditional source of recognized college credit. Among the examinations covered are the American College Testing Proficiency Examination Program: Regents College Examinations (ACT-PEP: RCEs), the College Level Examination Program (CLEP), and the Defense Activity for Non-Traditional Education Support (DANTES) examinations. These testing methods are the best known and most widely used programs for gaining college credit through nontraditional methods. Other testing systems include the Graduate Record Examinations (GREs), Thomas Edison College Examination Program (TECEP), Ohio University Testing Course Credit by Examination (CCE), Advanced Placement (AP) Examinations, and New York University (NYU) Foreign Language Proficiency Tests. Except for the GREs, these testing systems are not widely available to soldiers and are not detailed in this book. Additional information on these systems can be obtained at the military education center.

HOW ARE THESE TESTS DEVELOPED,
AND ARE THEY VALID?
The major goal of these examinations is to measure learning in a subject area, regardless of the method used, against the same standard of learning gained from a college classroom. A standard practice in developing these tests is to administer them to a sample of college and university students who are completing equivalent courses. This way, the achievement levels

on the tests can be compared directly with the achievement of college students who have completed the course for which credit is intended. This process of nationally norming the examinations ensures their validity and reliability and provides data for determining the passing score of each test.

ARE THERE ANY PREREQUISITES
FOR TAKING THESE EXAMINATIONS?
None of the testing programs addressed on the following pages has any prerequisites. Keep in mind, however, that these tests are designed to measure knowledge that you gained outside the traditional classroom. It is unlikely that you could get lucky and pass a test with no prior learning of the subject. Some education centers, in an attempt to keep soldiers from trying to get lucky on a test, now require them to take a pretest. If a soldier does not score high enough on the pretest to justify taking the real test, the ESO often recommends a study plan. It may be necessary to register for these examinations several days in advance at some education centers.

HOW MUCH DO THESE TESTS COST?
All examinations for college credit detailed in this chapter are free to active-duty military personnel.

WHERE CAN YOU TAKE THESE EXAMINATIONS?
All the examinations listed can be taken at your AEC. To find the nearest military education center, consult the appendixes in the back of this book. Appendixes D and E provide complete lists of all known permanent military education centers throughout the world.

WHAT KIND OF COLLEGE CREDIT
CAN YOU GET FOR THESE TESTS?
Each examination offered through ACT-PEP, CLEP, and DANTES is listed on the following pages, along with the ACE college credit recommendations for that test. These examinations cover a wide variety of topics, and their content is based on material covered in equivalent college courses. Tests can be taken to earn college credit in courses ranging from Statistics to the Fundamentals of Electronics to the Civil War and Reconstruction to Microbiology. The tests themselves, however, do not award college credit; a student must have his or her official test results forwarded to the school from which college credit is being sought. That school then evaluates the

test results and awards the appropriate credit based on the ACE recommendations and its own policies.

WHICH SCHOOLS AWARD CREDIT FOR THESE EXAMINATIONS?

Two of the schools detailed in this book, Regents College and Thomas Edison State College, accept all ACE recommendations for awarding college credit. All other schools listed in this book accept most ACE recommendations for awarding college credit for examinations. To determine the acceptability of a specific testing program at a particular school, soldiers should see their ESOs and ask to see the *Servicemembers Opportunity Colleges Guide*. This guide has over 1,000 pages of schools that work closely with military personnel and details which testing programs are accepted at each of these institutions. Servicemember Opportunity Colleges are covered in Chapter 10. Most schools also publish the acceptability of college credit examinations in their catalogs.

HOW ARE GRADES ASSIGNED FOR THESE EXAMINATIONS?

Examinations for college credit are assigned a numerical score. Some schools convert this numerical score to a letter grade. Most schools, however, annotate a passing numerical score with a "P" on the college transcript. For those examinations in which a passing score was not obtained, most schools simply make no annotation on the transcript. In other words, if one passes the examination, it is placed on the college transcript; if one fails, it is not. Those institutions that do convert passing numerical scores to traditional letter grades maintain their own conversion scales. Specific institutions should be contacted to determine whether they use a conversion system and, if so, the specific grade ranges. The following sample score range conversions for CLEP Subject Examinations are used by Regents College:

CLEP Title	A	B	C
Accounting, Introductory	56–80	50–55	47–49
Human Growth and Development	55–80	49–54	45–48
Marketing, Principles of	58–80	53–57	50–52

Unlike other examinations, the ACT-PEP: RCEs with extended response sections are already reported as letter grades. For these examinations, the numerical scores are converted to letter grades according to the following scale:

Grade	Range of Scores
A	63–80
B	56–62
C	45–55

ACT-PEP: RCEs

What Are the Different Tests Offered Through ACT-PEP: RCEs?
There are over thirty-five college-level ACT-PEP: Regents College Examinations (RCEs) in the series. Although most of these examinations are multiple-choice tests, some are essay tests. These examinations are offered in the arts and sciences, business, education, and nursing and are listed below:

Test Title	Recommended Credit	Minimum Score
Arts and Sciences		
Abnormal Psychology	3 SH (U)	45
American Dream (Part I) (E)	6 SH (U)	45
Anatomy and Physiology	6 SH (L)	45
Foundations of Gerontology	3 SH (U)	45
History of Nazi Germany (E)	3 SH (U)	45
International Conflicts in the Twentieth Century (E)	3 SH (U)	45
Microbiology	3 SH (U)	45
New Rule of Reason: Philosophy and Society in the Seventeenth Century (E)	3 SH (U)	45
Religions of the World (E)	3 SH (U)	45
Statistics	3 SH (L)	45
War in Vietnam (1945–1975): A Global Perspective (E)	3 SH (U)	45
Business		
Business Policy and Strategy	3 SH (U)	45

Test Title	Recommended Credit	Minimum Score
Corporation Finance	3 SH (U)	45
Human Resource Management and Strategy	3 SH (U)	45
Introductory Accounting	6 SH (L)	45
Labor Relations	3 SH (U)	45
Organizational Behavior	3 SH (U)	45
Principles of Management	3 SH (L)	45
Principles of Marketing	3 SH (L)	45
Production/Operations Management	3 SH (U)	45
Education		
Reading in the Elementary School	6 SH (L)	45
Nursing		
Adult Nursing	8 SH (U)	45
Commonalities in Nursing Care (2 tests)		
Area A	5 SH (L)	45
Area B	5 SH (L)	45
Differences in Nursing Care (3 tests)		
Area A	5 SH (L)	45
Area B	5 SH (L)	45
Area C	5 SH (L)	45
Fundamentals of Nursing	8 SH (L)	45
Health Restoration (2 tests)		
Health Restoration I	4 SH (U)	45
Health Restoration II	4 SH (U)	45
Health Support (2 tests)		
Health Support I	4 SH (U)	45
Health Support II	4 SH (U)	45
Maternal and Child Nursing (2 tests)	8 SH (U)	45
Maternity Nursing	3 SH (L)	45
Occupational Strategies in Nursing	3 SH (L)	45
Professional Strategies in Nursing	4 SH (U)	45
Psychiatric/Mental Health Nursing	8 SH (U)	45

E, essay examination
SH, semester hours of college credit
L, recommended for lower-division baccalaureate credit
U, recommended for upper-division baccalaureate credit

What Is the Difference Between Lower- and Upper-Division Baccalaureate Credit?

All college credit applied toward a four-year bachelor's degree is classified as either lower- or upper-division credit. Lower-division credit is awarded for general knowledge or for courses normally taken during the first or second year of college. Most introductory and intermediate courses and knowledge, or courses taken at a community or two-year college, are recognized for lower-division credit. Lower-division courses normally begin with the number 1 or 2. For example, freshman English Composition may be numbered ENG 101 or ENG 1015.

Upper-division credit is awarded for advanced knowledge or for courses normally taken during the third and fourth years of college. Such courses and knowledge are normally more intensive than lower-division ones and often have prerequisites. Upper-division courses normally begin with the number 3 or 4. For example, a senior-level history course such as Special Research Topics in History may be numbered HIS 460 or HIS 4521.

What Is Covered in the ACT-PEP Essay Tests?

Following is a brief description of the type of knowledge tested in each of the ACT-PEP essay examinations. This information can be used as a guide when studying.

American Dream (Part I): This test reflects an interdisciplinary course of study that examines both the conflict and the consensus that resulted as groups and individuals struggled to define and shape the American dream prior to the Civil War. It draws from U.S. literature, history, and political science.

History of Nazi Germany: This test reflects a study of the history of post-World War I Germany through World War II. It includes the rise of the National Socialists to power, aspects of life in Nazi Germany, foreign policy, and war and society from 1939 to 1945.

International Conflicts in the Twentieth Century: This test reflects a study of the origins of the great international conflicts of the twentieth century and their relevance to ongoing efforts to maintain international security in the post-Cold War era.

New Rule of Reason: Philosophy and Society in the Seventeenth Century: This test reflects an interdisciplinary course of study of seventeenth-century western European philosophy viewed in the context of four major social changes: capitalism, modern science, the nation-state, and challenges to religious dogma. The content of this test is based on the writings of philosophers of the period and on selected modern critical interpretations.

Religions of the World: This test reflects an interdisciplinary course of study of the major religions as viewed in their social and historical context. This test requires a general knowledge of the concepts drawn from sociology, psychology, and philosophy. The individual should be able to analyze and compare the various religious beliefs and practices.

War in Vietnam (1945-1975): A Global Perspective: This test reflects a study of the war in Vietnam from the conflict's beginnings in Vietnamese culture to the aftermath of communist victory in 1975. The test focuses on three major themes: the role of culture, the temporal and international context of the war, and conflicting interpretations of the war.

How Can You Prepare for ACT-PEP Multiple-Choice Tests?

All the ACT-PEP examinations have corresponding informational study guides that provide an overview of each test. Depending on supply, the ESO at the military education center may provide these materials. Otherwise, soldiers can call Regents College at (518) 464-8500 or ACT-PEP at (319) 337-1363 and request the free study guides. They also contain information about the optional purchase or rental of audio- and videotapes and books designed to assist with test preparation.

COLLEGE LEVEL EXAMINATION PROGRAM (CLEP)

What Are the Different Tests Offered Through CLEP?

There are two types of CLEP tests: CLEP General Examinations and CLEP Subject Examinations. Both types are detailed and listed below.

CLEP General Examinations measure college-level achievement in five basic areas of liberal arts: English composition, humanities, mathematics, natural sciences, and social sciences and history. The test questions on the general examinations relate to material usually presented in the first two years of a college curriculum. These examinations are as follows:

CLEP GENERAL EXAMINATIONS

Form Number	Test Title	Recommended Credit	Minimum Score
Test 1 General	English Composition (without essay)	6 SH (L)	421
Test 2 General	Social Sciences and History	6 SH (L)	421
Test 3 General	Natural Sciences	6 SH (L)	421
Test 4 General	Humanities	6 SH (L)	421
Test 5 General	Mathematics	6 SH (L)	421
Test 6 General	English Composition (with essay)	6 SH (L)	421

SH, semester hours of college credit
L, recommended for lower-division baccalaureate credit

CLEP Subject Examinations measure college-level learning for specific college courses. These tests measure knowledge of basic concepts, principles, relationships, and applications involved in college courses with similar titles. These tests are as follows:

CLEP SUBJECT EXAMINATIONS

Form Number	Test Title	Recommended Credit	Minimum Score
TG 001	American Government	3 SH (L)	47
TC 003	American Literature (E)	6 SH (L)	46
TD 004	Analysis and Interpretation of Literature (E)	6 SH (L)	49

CLEP SUBJECT EXAMINATIONS

Form Number	Test Title	Recommended Credit	Minimum Score
TG 006	College Algebra	3 SH (L)	46
TC 007	College Algebra-Trigonometry	3 SH (L)	45
TD 012	English Literature (E)	6 SH (L)	46
TG 013	General Chemistry	6 SH (L)	47
TG 014	Introductory Psychology	3 SH (L)	47
TE 017	Human Growth and Development	3 SH (L)	45
TE 018	Principles of Management	3 SH (L)	46
TG 019	Introductory Accounting	6 SH (L)	47
TE 020	Introductory Business Law	3 SH (L)	51
TF 023	Principles of Marketing I	3 SH (L)	50
TB 028	Trigonometry	3 SH (L)	50
TE 036	Principles of Macroeconomics	3 SH (L)	44
TD 037	Principles of Microeconomics	3 SH (L)	41
TG 039	Introductory Sociology	3 SH (L)	47
TC 050	French: Levels 1 and 2 (T)		
	Second Semester	6 SH (L)	39
	Fourth Semester	12 SH (L)	45
TD 051	German: Levels 1 and 2 (T)		
	Second Semester	6 SH (L)	36
	Fourth Semester	12 SH (L)	42
TE 052	Spanish: Levels 1 and 2 (T)		
	Second Semester	6 SH (L)	41
	Fourth Semester	12 SH (L)	50
TC 053	Calculus with Elementary Functions (C)	6 SH (L)	41
TE 054	General Biology	6 SH (L)	46
TA 055	American History I	3 SH (L)	45
TC 056	American History II	3 SH (L)	45
TD 057	Western Civilization I	3 SH (L)	46
TE 058	Western Civilization II	3 SH (L)	47

CLEP SUBJECT EXAMINATIONS

Form Number	Test Title	Recommended Credit	Minimum Score
TB 059	Introduction to Educational Psychology	3 SH (L)	47
TA 060	Information Systems and Computer Applications	3 SH (L)	52
TA 061	Freshman College Composition (E)	6 SH (L)	44

E, optional essay section available
C, use of a scientific calculator permitted, but programmable calculators and calculators that can display graphs not permitted; all calculator memories must be cleared before beginning the examination
T, examination includes both cassette tape and booklet
SH, semester hours of college credit
L, recommended for lower-division baccalaureate credit

How Can You Prepare for CLEP Examinations?

Just like ACT-PEP examinations, all CLEPs have free informational study guides that provide an overview of each test. Most ESOs at military education centers normally have a large supply of these pamphlets. If the materials are unavailable at the military education center, they can be requested by mail or phone at CLEP, PO Box 6600, Princeton, NJ 08541-6600; telephone (609) 951-1026.

DEFENSE ACTIVITY FOR NON-TRADITIONAL EDUCATION SUPPORT (DANTES)

What Are The Different Tests Offered Through the DSST Program?

The DANTES Subject Standardized Test (DSST) program is an extensive series of examinations in college and technical subjects. These tests are comparable to the final examinations in the equivalent college courses. The examinations are as follows:

DANTES SUBJECT STANDARDIZED TEST

Form Number	Test Title	Recommended Credit	Minimum Score
Mathematics			
SE 424	Introductory College Algebra	3 SH (L)	46
SE 450	Principles of Statistics	3 SH (L)	48
Social Science			
SE 461	Art of the Western World	3 SH (L)	48
SE 465	Contemporary Western Europe: 1946–1990	3 SH (L)	48
SE 469	An Introduction to the Modern Middle East	3 SH (L)	44
SF 470	Human/Cultural Geography	3 SH (L)	48
SF 473	A History of the Vietnam War	3 SH (L)	49
SE 483	The Civil War and Reconstruction	3 SH (U)	47
SE 489	Foundations of Education	3 SH (L)	46
SF 490	Lifespan Developmental Psychology	3 SH (L)	46
SF 494	General Anthropology	3 SH (L)	47
SG 497	Introduction to Law Enforcement	3 SH (L)	45
SF 498	Criminal Justice	3 SH (L)	49
SF 562	Fundamentals of Counseling	3 SH (L)	47
Business			
SF 524	Principles of Finance	3 SH (U)	46
SF 525	Principles of Financial Accounting	3 SH (L)	49
SE 528	Introductory Cost Accounting (D)	3 SH (U)	46
SE 529	Auditing I (D)	3 SH (U)	47

DANTES SUBJECT STANDARDIZED TEST

Form Number	Test Title	Recommended Credit	Minimum Score
SF 530	Personnel/Human Resource Management	3 SH (L)	48
SF 531	Organizational Behavior	3 SH (L)	48
SE 532	Principles of Supervision	3 SH (L)	46
SE 534	Business Law II	3 SH (U)	52
SE 536	Introduction to Computers with Programming in BASIC	3 SH (L)	47
SE 543	Introduction to Business	3 SH (L)	46
SG 548	Money and Banking	3 SH (U)	48
SE 550	Personal Finance	3 SH (L)	46
SE 551	Management Information Systems	3 SH (U)	46
SE 812	Business Mathematics	3 SH (L)	45
Physical Science			
SF 500	Astronomy	3 SH (L)	48
SF 508	Here's to Your Health	3 SH (L)	48
SF 511	Environment and Humanity: The Race to Save the Planet	3SH (L)	46
SE 512	Principles of Physical Science I	3 SH (L)	47
SF 519	Physical Geology	3 SH (L)	46
Foreign Language			
SG579	Beginning German I (D)	3 SH (L)	45
SG580	Beginning German II (D)	3 SH (L)	45
SF583	Beginning Spanish I (D)	3 SH (L)	48
SF584	Beginning Spanish II (D)	3 SH (L)	46
SE 585	Beginning Italian I (D)	3 SH (L)	46
Applied Technology			
SF 740	Basic Automotive Service (D)	3 SH (TC)	46
SE 756	Introduction to Carpentry (D)	3 SH (TC)	49
SE 770	Basic Technical Drafting (D)	3 SH (TC)	48
SE 782	Fundamentals of Electronics (D)	3 SH (TC)	45
SF 788	Electric Circuits (D)	6 SH (TC)	46

DANTES SUBJECT STANDARDIZED TEST

Form Number	Test Title	Recommended Credit	Minimum Score
SF 820	Technical Writing	3 SH (L)	46
SE 935	Principles of Refrigeration Technology (D)	3 SH (TC)	45
Humanities			
SF 474	Ethics in America	3 SH (L)	46
SE 496	Introduction to World Religions	3 SH (L)	49
SE 821-826	Principles of Public Speaking	3 SH (L)	47 (S)

SH, semester hours of college credit

L, recommended for lower-division baccalaureate credit

U, recommended for upper-division baccalaureate credit

D, discontinued as of December 31, 1996, but included for clarification because the test lists of military education centers are sometimes outdated

TC, in addition to credit in a lower-division baccalaureate program, also recommended for credit toward some technical degree programs

S, examinee must also receive a passing grade on a tape-recorded speech

How Can You Prepare for DANTES Tests?

As with the ACT-PEPs and CLEPs, DANTES examinations have free informational study guides that can be obtained through the military education center. Materials can also be requested by mail or phone at DANTES Program Office, Educational Testing Service, Princeton, NJ 08541-0001; telephone (609) 951-6425. Another excellent tool that can assist in preparing for DANTES examinations is the Annenberg Program.

What Is the Annenberg Program?

The Annenberg Program was begun by DANTES in 1989 to help military personnel prepare for certain DANTES college credit examinations. The program initially used audio and videotaped college courses, along with textbooks and study guides, to prepare personnel for specific examinations. DANTES has since discontinued the use of audio- and videotapes to prepare for specific examinations. Students are still allowed to use all existing tapes to prepare for college credit tests, resident courses, and independent study courses, but the new tests no longer correlate directly with any of the existing tapes.

Is the Annenberg Program Worthwhile?
The Annenberg Program is a valuable educational tool that is well worth the time. Colleges that use videos believe that they enhance and supplement the more traditional instructional methods. Experienced test takers often use the knowledge gained in one course or test to prepare for related examinations. Overlapping knowledge is essential to education, and success often requires the use of many resources. The Annenberg Program is one of these resources. The Annenberg materials continue to serve as valuable learning tools to supplement knowledge gained through resident courses, independent study courses, or informal learning at home. For these reasons, most AECs keep Annenberg Program materials and tapes in their libraries.

What Other Video-Based College Courses Are Available?
There are many video-based college courses available. Soldiers specifically seeking video-based instruction can consult the undergraduate section of the *DANTES External Degree Catalog*. Approximately 75 percent of the schools listed provide video-based courses. In addition, the *DANTES Independent Study Catalog* lists over 250 college credit-by-examination courses, many of which offer video-based instruction. In addition to the AEC, most military and civilian libraries have audiovisual materials related to college credit-by-examination topics.

GRADUATE RECORD EXAMINATIONS (GRES)

What Kind of Testing System Is the GRE?
GREs are designed to assess the comprehensive undergraduate competence of students after four years of college study. There are two types of GREs: the General GRE and the GRE Subject Tests.

The General GRE is designed to measure verbal, quantitative, and analytical skills acquired after many years of learning and is generally associated with attendance at a graduate school. These skills are not directly related to any specific field of study.

GRE Subject Tests measure achievement in specific fields of study, such as knowledge gained in an undergraduate major or mastery of the concepts, principles, and knowledge basic to success in specific graduate fields.

What GRE Subject Examinations Are Available?
The GRE Subject Examinations are as follows:
Biochemistry
Biology
Chemistry
Computer Science
Economics
Revised Education
Engineering
Geology
History
Literature in English
Mathematics
Music
Physics
Political Science
Psychology
Sociology

Do Schools Award College Credit for These Examinations
Most schools do not award college credit for completion of the General
GRE, and it is not covered in this book. Some schools do, however, award
college credit for GRE Subject Examinations. Regents College and
Thomas Edison State College, for example, award up to 30 semester hours
of college credit in a particular discipline for successful completion of the
corresponding GRE Subject Examination.

How Do Colleges Determine How Much Credit Is Awarded?
Each school has its own policies governing how much credit it awards for
each examination. The most credit that is awarded for any examination,
however, is 30 semester hours. Normally, 15 semester hours are granted in
lower-level college work, and 15 are granted in upper-level college work.
Some schools, such as Regents College, have implemented a graduated
scale so that a student is granted more credit with increased levels of performance on the GRE Subject Examinations. It is likely that all schools
will eventually adopt this same graduated-scale approach to granting credit
for the GRE Subject Exams. Although only a high score will result in the
awarding of all 30 semester hours, a passing but below-average score will
result in the awarding of at least 3 semester hours. The higher you score,
the more semester hours the school will award you.

How Much Do These Tests Cost?

All GREs are free to soldiers. However, soldiers who decide to retake any GRE to improve their scores must pay for the retest unless the tests are taken in different fiscal years.

How Are the Tests Scored?

The GREs Subject Exams are scored on a scale of 200 to 990 points. The actual range of scores for a particular test is always much smaller, however, because no one ever answers all the questions correctly. The high scores may be as low as 700. The scores vary widely for each exam, but the scores alone have little meaning without the percentile marks. The percentile mark indicates how well the examinee scored in relation to others who took the same test. A score of 700 may be in the 99th percentile on one GRE Subject Exam but in the 68th percentile on another.

When and Where Are the GRE Subject Examinations Administered

All GREs are administered on selected national test dates (usually once per quarter) at most military education centers (see Appendixes D and E for the nearest location). Soldiers must usually make appointments several weeks or months in advance. Since there are limited test dates in a year and a limit to the number of examinees that the test proctor is allowed to monitor, there is always more demand than supply. When making your schedule, call and check on the next national test date and reserve your seat for the GRE at the same time.

How Can You Obtain More Information About GRE Subject Examinations

Additional information can be obtained by contacting GRE at Graduate Record Examination, Educational Testing Service, PO Box 6000, Princeton, NJ 08541-6000; telephone (609) 771-7670.

7

DANTES
Distance Learning Programs

DANTES distance learning is the heart of nontraditional education. It allows soldiers to take college, technical, or vocational courses from accredited U.S. colleges and universities using combinations of textbook reading, correspondence study, videotapes, computer networks and conferencing, and classes delivered by satellite or cable. DANTES distance learning programs allow soldiers to take a single course or complete an entire degree program. Using these programs, soldiers can actually earn an associate's, bachelor's, or even master's degree, and most require no classroom attendance. These nontraditional programs are perfect for many soldiers who cannot attend traditional college classes due to work schedules, remote duty locations, and deployments.

WHAT KINDS OF PROGRAMS ARE AVAILABLE?
There are three different programs available: the DANTES External Degree Program, the Independent Study Program, and the Distance Education and Training Council Program.

WHAT IS THE PURPOSE OF EACH OF THESE PROGRAMS?
The DANTES Independent Study Program allows soldiers to pursue a variety of individual college courses. The *DANTES Independent Study Catalog* provides soldiers with more than 6,000 high school, undergraduate, graduate, and examination preparation correspondence courses from which to choose. All the courses are offered by regionally accredited institutions.

The DANTES External Degree Program makes available degree programs from fifty accredited colleges and universities that have few or no residency requirements for degree completion. With this program, soldiers can earn an Associate of Arts (AA), Associate of Science (AS), Bachelor of Arts (BA), Bachelor of Science (BS), Master of Arts (MA), or Master of Science (MS) degree. Soldiers also have access to the member colleges of the Mind Extension University (MEU), which allows soldiers to earn AA, AS, BA, BS, MA, and MS degrees via cable television, satellite television, and videotape. The *DANTES External Degree Catalog* lists approximately 100 associate, 225 baccalaureate, 100 graduate, and 45 credit-bearing certificate programs.

The DANTES Distance Education and Training Council (DETC) Program allows soldiers to take vocational, technical, and some nontechnical courses. The *DETC Catalog* contains course listings of all accredited schools and provides a means of independent study for those who want to earn associate's, bachelor's, and master's degrees in vocational programs.

ARE THE SCHOOLS THAT PARTICIPATE IN THESE PROGRAMS "REAL SCHOOLS" WITH GOOD REPUTATIONS?

There are over forty schools that participate in the DANTES Independent Study Program and fifty schools that participate in the DANTES External Degree Program. All these schools are fully accredited institutions, and most are well known. There are also several schools that participate in the DANTES DETC Program. Complete lists of these institutions follow.

DANTES Independent Study Institutions

Arizona State University	Oregon State System
Brigham Young University	of Higher Education
The College of West Virginia	Pennsylvania State University
Embry-Riddle Aeronautical	Southwest Texas State
University	Syracuse University
Indiana University	Texas Tech University
Mississippi State University	Thomas Edison State College
Ohio University	University of Alabama
Oklahoma State University	University of Alaska–Fairbanks

University of Arizona
University of Arkansas
University of California
  Extension
University of Idaho
University of Illinois
University of Kansas
University of Kentucky
University of Minnesota
University of Mississippi
University of Missouri
University of Nebraska–
  Lincoln
University of Nevada–Reno
University of North Carolina
University of North Dakota

University of Northern
  Iowa
University of Oklahoma
University of South Carolina
University of Southern
  Mississippi
University of Tennessee
University of Utah
University of Washington
University of Wisconsin
University of Wyoming
Utah State University
Washington State University
Western Kentucky
  University

DANTES External Degree Institutions

Auburn University
Boise State University
California State University–
  Dominguez Hills
Charter Oak State College
City Colleges of Chicago
City University
The College of West Virginia
Colorado State University
Defiance College
Embry-Riddle Aeronautical
  University
Empire State College
George Washington University
Georgia Institute of Technology
Governors State University
Graceland College
Indiana Institute of Technology
Indiana University

Kansas State University
Liberty University
Mind Extension University
National Technological
  University
Norwich University
Ohio University
Pennsylvania State University
Pikes Peak Community
  College
Regents College
Regis University
Rochester Institute
  Technology
Roger Williams University
Saint Joseph's College
Salve Regina College
Scott Community College

Seattle Central Community College
Southern Methodist University
Syracuse University
Thomas Edison State College
United States Sports Academy
University of Alabama
University of Arkansas
(College of Engineering)
University of Cincinnati
University of Colorado
at Colorado Springs

University of Idaho
(College of Engineering)
University of Iowa
University of Maryland
University of Phoenix
University of Southern
Colorado
Upper Iowa University
Vincennes University
Washington State University
Western Illinois University

DANTES DETC Institutions
American Academy of Nutrition
American College of Prehospital Medicine
American Health Information Management Association
American Military University
Berean University
California College for Health Sciences
Catholic Distance University
Cleveland Institute of Electronics
Educational Institute of the American Hotel and Motel Association
Grantham College of Engineering
ICI University
International Correspondence Schools
Modern Schools of America
National Tax Training School
Peoples College of Independent Study
World College

HOW ARE COURSES DELIVERED?
Schools participating in these programs use a variety of methods, from low-tech "snail mail" to high-tech electronic mail (E-mail), to deliver educational choices aimed at individual students around the world. Students still use the traditional textbooks, pen, and paper, but many are simultane-

ously exploiting the speed and efficiency of advancing technology to increase educational opportunities and decrease both course and degree completion times. Most schools now have web sites on the Internet, and many utilize E-mail to submit and receive course lessons and papers or to communicate directly with instructors. Using the Internet, students can send their assignments directly from their own computers at home to the instructor's computer in the school in a matter of seconds. Other schools use other high-tech methods such as video teletraining, whereby courses are taught via cable or satellite television. For the DANTES schools with technology-supported programs, see last section of this chapter.

ARE THESE PROGRAMS DESIGNED FOR EVERYONE?
These programs are designed to meet the needs of military personnel who have an educational goal and are willing to work for it. These programs were not designed for those who lack discipline and persistence. Those who succeed in these programs have academic and emotional maturity, specific educational goals, the ability to work alone, the capacity for self-starting, self-understanding and self-motivation, persistence, and self-confidence.

WHAT ARE THE BENEFITS
OF USING DISTANCE LEARNING PROGRAMS?
With these programs, soldiers can earn credit wherever they are stationed, whether it is Fort Drum, New York, or Camp Casey, Korea, or Fort Hood, Texas. These programs and materials are portable, so soldiers can study when their schedules permit or when they want to. These programs are approved for tuition assistance, and, like all programs detailed in this book, they can enhance promotion potential, assist in retirement preparation, and lead to better-paying jobs.

ARE THERE ANY SPECIAL REQUIREMENTS
THAT MUST BE COMPLETE BEFORE ENROLLING?
Check with the school; some courses and degree programs have prerequisites or other requirements that must be met prior to enrolling.

HOW MANY COURSES CAN YOU TAKE AT ONE TIME?
The only limits are those that you impose on yourself, but be realistic. Education counselors normally recommend one course to start, until you

get your feet wet. There may also be budget constraints that dictate how many courses for which you can be reimbursed. Listen to your education counselor.

HOW DO YOU ENROLL?

Make an appointment with a counselor at your local military education center. After asking you about your educational goals, the education counselor will assist you in selecting the appropriate courses to pursue your goals. These counselors have valuable experience, knowledge, and access to materials that can be helpful in choosing the appropriate school. The counselor will then help you complete the DANTES Distance Learning Enrollment Form (DANTES 1562/31). Mail the first two copies, signed by you and your counselor or other certifying official, with the total payment or credit card number to cover tuition, fees, and book costs directly to the school. DANTES will reimburse you only if this form is used. Some schools also require that students complete the school enrollment form.

HOW MUCH TUITION ASSISTANCE WILL YOU RECEIVE?

Depending on the budget requirements for the fiscal year, possible specified dollar limits, and the availability of funding, soldiers are reimbursed for up to 75 percent of the tuition costs. No lab, special, or textbook fees are reimbursed. Soldiers should always speak with their counselors to clarify current tuition assistance funding levels before registering for a course. Unlike with other college courses, Army personnel (active duty and National Guard) must pay all distance learning costs at enrollment. After successfully completing the course, soldiers are reimbursed.

Check with your education counselor about tuition assistance for DETC schools; most, but not all, courses offered by DETC schools are approved for tuition assistance.

MUST YOU PAY TUITION IN ADVANCE,
OR CAN YOU MAKE INSTALLMENT PAYMENTS?

Some schools have plans that allow for installment payments. These installment plans are an agreement between the student and the school. The student must pay all costs before the school will issue a grade report, and tuition reimbursement cannot be made until the school issues a grade report. If you are considering enrolling, be sure to ask the school about refund policies before enrolling or before signing a contract. Many

schools also permit payment by credit card. When paying by credit card, use the space for the card number on the DANTES Distance Learning Enrollment Form and be sure that the school accepts the type of credit card you are using.

WHAT OTHER ITEMS MUST YOU PAY FOR?
All books and fees are paid for by the student, and the Army does not reimburse soldiers for these expenses. Soldiers also pay the postage for materials sent to the distance learning school. The school pays postage on materials sent to the student.

HOW DOES REIMBURSEMENT WORK?
If the student is in the Army or Navy, DANTES processes the reimbursement upon successful completion of the course for schools listed in the DANTES catalogs. The school sends DANTES a grade report within thirty days of course completion. DANTES processes the application and adds the accounting data, and the paperwork is sent to the Defense Accounting Office. The soldier receives a check in the mail from the Defense Accounting Office within six to eight weeks after course completion. If you are going to be reimbursed through DANTES, be sure to provide the schools and DANTES with all address changes as soon as possible. Government checks cannot be forwarded and will be returned by the Post Office to the Defense Accounting Office. Soldiers can also elect to be reimbursed by direct deposit. With direct deposit, reimbursement time can be cut by as much as two to four weeks. Directions for using direct deposit reimbursement and samples of forms can be obtained from your local education center.

USE OF TECHNOLOGY
IN DANTES DISTANCE LEARNING PROGRAMS
The following summaries describe the use of technology in some of the DANTES distance learning programs. Although the list is partial, it demonstrates how many schools have successfully integrated the latest technology into their learning programs.

Auburn University
The Graduate Outreach Program at Auburn University serves students primarily with videotapes of classroom lectures. These tapes are made live each quarter and mailed directly to the students. Many professors use E-

mail to communicate with students, and some use html pages or url addresses to post material and assignments on the World Wide Web (WWW).

Boise State University
Boise State University (BSU) offers a fully accredited, totally nonresident MS degree in instructional and performance technology (IPT) via asynchronous (non-real-time) computer conferencing. Students call a toll-free number and participate in class discussion, submit course assignments, take tests, register, and even order course materials via the BSU-IPT online computer conferencing system. To enroll in a course, a student must own a computer and modem that meet program specifications and submit a Graduate Admissions Form and a completed Equipment Availability Checklist. The degree requirements consist of twenty-one required courses and fifteen electives, with approximately four different courses offered each semester.

Brigham Young University
Brigham Young University (BYU) independent study allows students to register for courses on the WWW. It also offers a unique feature called "GradeCheck." This system allows students and counselors to access grades and scores on assignments. In addition to these offerings, BYU is currently working on several courses that can be delivered completely over the WWW or on computer disks.

California State University–Dominguez Hills External Degree
This on-line program has eleven courses that offer students with computers the option of using the WWW to see the same materials they get in print with regular courses, including the syllabi, lecture notes, schedule, and instructions for the course. The WWW also links the students to other sites with material or research information related to the courses. Eighty percent of the instructors have E-mail, and many of them allow students to use it to communicate with them. Some instructors also allow lessons to be submitted via E-mail.

Embry-Riddle Aeronautical University
The Embry-Riddle Aeronautical University Graduate Program allows students to interact electronically with faculty, staff, and fellow students via a private forum on CompuServe (accessed through the Internet). Synchronous and asynchronous communications are available. Assignments and

feedback are provided by the professors via private E-mail. Questions are transmitted by the student to the forum and posted on the bulletin board for other students to review and capture the professor's response. The Embry-Riddle forum is accessible from more than 185 countries.

Governors State University

Governors State University (GSU) students can join a listserv discussion group once a week and submit assignments via E-mail. (Listserv, also known as list servers, is a form of computer conferencing that uses a program to automatically redistribute E-mail to all users on a mailing list.) Many of the television and correspondence courses have an E-mail component for those with computer access. Students in the Board of Governors BA degree program can use these media-based courses, as well as experiential learning by portfolio and credit transferred from regionally accredited institutions, to complete the required 15 hours at GSU. Information about courses and programs is available from the GSU home page on the WWW.

Indiana University

Students enrolled in most independent study courses at Indiana University can communicate with their instructors via E-mail. When course materials permit it, students can also submit lessons and receive grades for them by E-mail. Students in some courses can access course materials over the WWW, and more WWW courses are under development.

Kansas State University

The Division of Continuing Education at Kansas State University offers five courses that use a combination of media to deliver course content to students. These courses use computer conferencing (listserv) to emphasize interaction between faculty and students, as well as collaborative learning. In addition, audio teleconferencing is used for monthly real-time class sessions for discussion, question-and-answer periods, and review and to supplement videotapes, audiotapes and print materials.

National Technological University

National Technological University uses broadcast television, via satellite, to transmit MS degree courses in engineering and management from forty-seven leading U.S. universities to technical professionals directly at their places of employment. The Internet is used to facilitate student-faculty and student-student interaction through E-mail and WWW sites for homework, frequently asked questions (FAQs), and so forth. Students may also register for courses and apply for admission through the WWW.

Salve Regina University
Students may use the Internet to apply to Salve Regina University, register for courses, and submit course assignments. Students can also go on-line for asynchronous communication with instructors, other students, the extension study director, and staff. The university catalog, information guide, and faculty introductions are available on-line.

University of Alaska–Fairbanks
The Center for Distance Education, University of Alaska–Fairbanks, offers an on-line catalog of more than 100 courses available via correspondence study. Students can browse through the list of courses, view detailed descriptions of the courses, obtain a list of materials used in each course, or simply review how the independent study program works. Many instructors accept lessons by E-mail, and there are several on-line courses.

University of California Extension
The University of California Extension's on-line program offers twenty-five courses through America Online. The program combines asynchronous learning with real-time events—live chats with instructors and other students, as well as special live events. Assignments are sent to instructors via E-mail. Students and instructors may also communicate via bulletin boards, and they have access to electronic libraries and databases. Print copies of course guides and textbooks are used, and students still take paper exams with proctors.

University of Idaho Engineering Outreach Program
The University of Idaho Engineering Outreach courses are delivered primarily by videotape. The Internet is used to support distance teaching and learning. Engineering Outreach faculty use E-mail to communicate with students. Some faculty also establish on-line discussion groups so that students in a class can communicate with other students. Also, some faculty members make their course syllabi and notes available on the WWW.

University of Iowa

At the University of Iowa Guided Correspondence Study, students may use E-mail to send in any assignment that is plain text. Several courses offer the option of receiving responses via E-mail as well. Information about the Bachelor of Liberal Studies external degree program and Guided Correspondence Study (such as policies and course listings) is posted on WWW pages.

8

Regents College

Regents College, officially known as the University of the State of New York, Regents College, is probably one of the best-known and most utilized nontraditional postsecondary institutions in the United States. According to the Regents College Fact Sheet, the mission of Regents College is "founded on the belief that what someone knows is more important than where and how the knowledge was acquired. Regents College provides the opportunity for motivated adult learners to obtain recognition of their college-level educational achievement." Regents College also claims the distinction of being the "oldest and largest assessment and evaluation institution in the United States." It works in active partnership with colleges and universities, employers, health-care institutions, the U.S. military, and other organizations throughout the country to provide access to an affordable higher education experience. "While remaining open to all, the College assures academic integrity through rigorous requirements and careful assessment."*

HOW DOES REGENTS COLLEGE WORK?
Regents College offers twenty-six associate's and bachelor's degrees in liberal arts, business, nursing, and technology and has no campus residency requirement. The school also offers a master's degree in liberal arts. When students enroll, their prior college-level learning, both traditional classroom learning and many types of nontraditional learning, is evaluated for credit. The students then work with assigned academic advisers by phone and mail to determine the best route to completing their degrees. Students can complete degree requirements through a wide

*Information on Regents College has been taken from the Regents College Fact Sheet, Regents College Publication I#040329, and *Regents College Liberal Arts Catalog,* rev. ed. (Albany: University of the State of New York, March 1996).

variety of methods, including traditional college courses, accredited correspondence and other distance learning courses, military training and courses, selected on-the-job training, and accredited examinations for college credit. All these experiences are evaluated and consolidated on a single transcript.

WHAT TYPES OF STUDENTS EARN DEGREES THROUGH REGENTS COLLEGE?

Many Regents College graduates are people just like you, military personnel, working adults, or those with no access to traditional college resources. Regents College boasts that it "has over 19,000 enrolled students who live in every state in the United States and many foreign countries" and that approximately 4,500 students graduate each year. Regents College has awarded more than 64,000 degrees, and its graduates have high academic aspirations. Nearly three-quarters of them indicate that they expect to earn a master's or higher degree in their lifetime, and nearly 40 percent of the baccalaureate graduates pursue postgraduate study immediately after earning their Regents College degrees. The average age for a Regents College student is thirty-seven and over 81 percent of Regents College students are working adults employed full-time.

IS REGENTS COLLEGE ACCREDITED?

Regents College is accredited by the Middle States Association of Colleges and Schools, Commission on Higher Education. Regents College nursing degrees are accredited by the National League for Nursing. For a full list of accrediting institutions, see Appendix C.

WHAT ARE THE DIFFERENT TYPES OF DEGREES AND DEGREE PROGRAMS OFFERED BY REGENTS COLLEGE?

The following degrees are offered by Regents College:

Liberal Arts Degrees
Associate in Arts (requires 60 semester hours of credit, among other requirements)
Associate in Science (requires 60 semester hours of credit, among other requirements)
Bachelor of Arts (requires 120 semester hours of credit, which includes either two depth requirements of 12 semester credits each or

a single concentration option of 30 semester credits, among other
requirements)
Bachelor of Science (requires 120 semester hours of credit, which
includes either two depth requirements of 12 semester credits each
or a single concentration option of 30 semester credits, among other
requirements)
Master of Arts in Liberal Studies (requires 33 semester hours of grad-
uate-level credit and a thesis, among other requirements)
Students may pursue one of the following concentrations as part of
both the BS and BA degrees:
Area Studies (e.g., Latin America, Middle East)
Biology
Chemistry
Communication
Economics
Foreign Language and Literature (non-Western)
Foreign Language and Literature (Western)
Geography
Geology
History
Literature in English
Mathematics
Music
Philosophy
Physics
Political Science
Psychology
Sociology

Business Degrees
Associate in Science (Business)
Bachelor of Science in General Business
Bachelor of Science in Accounting (General)
Bachelor of Science in Accounting (NYS CPA track)
Bachelor of Science in Finance
Bachelor of Science in International Business
Bachelor of Science in Management of Human Resources
Bachelor of Science in Management of Information Systems
Bachelor of Science in Marketing
Bachelor of Science in Operations Management

Nursing Degrees
Associate in Applied Science (Nursing)
Associate in Science (Nursing)
Bachelor of Science (Nursing)

Technology Degrees
Associate in Science in Computer Science
Associate in Science in Electronics Technology
Associate in Science in Nuclear Technology
Associate in Science in Technology (with specialty)
Bachelor of Science in Computer Information Systems
Bachelor of Science in Computer Technology
Bachelor of Science in Electronics Technology
Bachelor of Science in Nuclear Technology
Bachelor of Science in Technology (with specialty)
Note: Not all specific requirements are detailed for Regents College degrees. Generally, all associate's degrees require 60 semester hours of credit in addition to other specific requirements. All bachelor's degrees require 120 semester hours of credit in addition to other specific requirements.

HOW MUCH DOES IT COST
TO EARN A DEGREE THROUGH REGENTS COLLEGE?
The cost of pursuing a degree through Regents College varies, depending on how long it takes a student to complete the degree. A student who completes a bachelor's degree within one year will pay approximately $1,000, and one who completes the same degree in two years will pay approximately $1,300. The cost of completing an associate's degree is approximately the same as the cost of a bachelor's degree. The fees normally increase modestly each September. Students should contact the school to obtain a specific fee schedule.

HOW CAN YOU OBTAIN MORE INFORMATION
ABOUT REGENTS COLLEGE?
To obtain more information about Regents College degrees, you can call Regents College at (518) 464-8500, or you can connect via modem

to the Regents College Bulletin Board System at (518) 464-8700. The bulletin board is accessible twenty-four hours a day, seven days a week. The modem settings are: no parity, 8 data bits, 1 stop bit, and the terminal setting is ANSI BBS or IBM PC. If you prefer to use regular mail, you can write to Regents College, University of the State of New York, 7 Columbia Circle, Albany, NY 12203-5159.

9

Thomas Edison State College

Thomas Edison State College, like Regents College, is one of the best known and most utilized nontraditional postsecondary institutions in the United States. According to the Thomas Edison State College Prospectus, the mission of the school is to provide "diverse and alternative methods of achieving a collegiate education of the highest quality for mature adults." Thomas Edison State College claims that it is "entirely devoted to the adult learner." The school is named after Thomas Alva Edison, who achieved college-level knowledge through independent research. Using distance education, the college enables adult learners to complete bachelor's and associate's degrees wherever they live and work. The college accepted its first students in the Master of Science in Management Degree Program in January 1996. Students in any state or nation can earn credit for college-level knowledge acquired outside the classroom, and Thomas Edison State College has no residency requirements.

HOW DOES THOMAS EDISON STATE COLLEGE WORK?

Thomas Edison State College (TESC) offers eleven bachelor's and associate's degrees in 119 different areas of study, a Master of Science in Management degree, and a wide range of nondegree and certificate programs. Upon enrollment, TESC students transfer an average of 30 to 60 semester hours to the school from other sources. After a student applies to a particular degree program, TESC assesses his or her learning and experiences and determines how close the student is to completing the desired degree. The student then enrolls and selects his or her preferred method or methods of completing the degree requirements. There are several degree completion options at TESC, including Portfolio Assessment, Distance and Independent Adult Learning (DIAL) Courses, (including Guided Study,

On-Line Computer Classroom, Contract Learning, and "Going the Distance"), Courses at Work and the Military, Credit for Certificates and Licenses, Transfer of Credit, and Approved Correspondence Courses.

WHAT TYPES OF STUDENTS EARN DEGREES THROUGH THOMAS EDISON STATE COLLEGE?

TESC has awarded more than 12,000 degrees to students worldwide, and it is designed exclusively for adult learners. Two-thirds of TESC's students are residents of New Jersey, and one-third are from other states and from about seventy foreign countries. The average age of TESC students is thirty-nine and 60 percent of them are enrolled in the bachelor's degree program. Although 40 percent earn associate's degrees, many are simultaneously enrolled in the bachelor's degree program.

IS THOMAS EDISON STATE COLLEGE ACCREDITED?

Thomas Edison State College is accredited by the Commission on Higher Education of the Middle States Association of Colleges and Schools. The Thomas Edison State College Nursing Program is accredited by the National League for Nursing.

WHAT ARE THE DIFFERENT TYPES OF DEGREES AND DEGREE PROGRAMS OFFERED BY THOMAS EDISON?

The following degrees are offered by Thomas Edison State College:

Liberal Arts Degrees

Associate in Arts (requires 60 semester hours of credit, among other requirements)

Associate in Science in Natural Sciences and Mathematics (requires 60 semester hours of credit, among other requirements)

Bachelor of Arts (requires 120 semester hours of credit, which includes either a concentration or a specialization, among other requirements)

Students may pursue one the following concentrations as part of the BA degrees (33 hours in three subject areas):

Humanities

Natural Sciences/Mathematics

Social Sciences/History

Students may pursue one the following specializations as part of the
BA degree (33 hours in one subject area):
African-American Studies
American Studies
Anthropology
Archaeology
Art
Asian Studies
Biology
Chemistry
Communications
Computer Science
Dance
Economics
Environmental Studies
Foreign Language
Geography
Geology
History
Journalism
Labor Studies
Literature
Mathematics
Music
Philosophy
Photography
Physics
Political Science
Psychology
Religion
Sociology
Theater Arts
Urban Studies
Women's Studies

Business and Management Degrees

Associate in Science in Management (requires 60 semester hours of
credit, among other requirements)
Bachelor of Science in Business Administration (requires 120 semester hours of credit, which includes a specialization, among other requirements)

Master of Science in Management (requires 42 semester hours of
graduate-level credit, among other requirements)
Students may pursue one of the following specializations as part
of the BS Business Administration degree (18 hours in one subject
area):
Accounting
Administrative Office Management
Advertising Management
Banking
Data Processing
Finance
General Management
Hospital Health Care Administration
Hotel/Motel/Restaurant Management
Human Resource Management
Insurance
International Business
Logistics
Marketing
Management Information Systems
Operations Management
Procurement
Public Administration
Purchasing and Materials
Real Estate
Retailing Management
School Business Administration
Transportation Management

Nursing Degrees
Bachelor of Science in Nursing (requires 120 semester hours of credit,
among other requirements; available only to registered nurses living
or working in New Jersey)

Applied Science and Technology
Associate in Science in Applied Science and Technology (requires 60
semester hours of credit, among other requirements)
Associate in Applied Science in Radiologic Technology (requires 60
semester hours, among other requirements)

Bachelor of Science in Applied Science and Technology (requires
120 semester hours of credit, which includes a specialization,
among other requirements)
Students may pursue one the following specializations as part of
the BS in Applied Science and Technology degree (33 hours in
one area):
Air Traffic Control*
Architectural Design
Aviation Flight Technology*
Aviation Maintenance*
Biomedical Electronics
Civil Engineering Technology
Clinical Laboratory Science*
Computer Science Technology
Construction
Dental Hygiene*
Diagnostic Imaging*
Electrical Technology
Electronics Engineering Technology
Engineering Graphics
Environmental Sciences
Fire Protection Science
Forestry
Horticulture
Laboratory Animal Science
Manufacturing Engineering Technology
Marine Engineering Technology
Mechanical Engineering Technology
Nondestructive Testing Technology
Nuclear Engineering Technology
Nuclear Medicine Technology*
Perfusion Technology*
Radiation Protection
Radiation Therapy*
Respiratory Care*
Surveying

*Students enrolled in these specializations must hold a professional certification.

Human and Social Services Degrees
Associate in Science in Public and Social Services (requires 60 semester hours of credit, among other requirements)
Bachelor of Science in Human Services (requires 120 semester hours of credit, which includes a specialization, among other requirements)
Students may pursue one the following specializations as part of the BS in Human Services degree (33 hours in one area):
Administration of Justice
Child Development Services
Community Services
Emergency Disaster Management
Gerontology
Health and Nutrition Counseling
Health Services
Health Services Administration
Health Services Education
Legal Services
Mental Health and Rehabilitative Services
Recreation Services
Social Services
Social Services Administration
Social Services for Special Populations

HOW MUCH DOES IT COST TO EARN A DEGREE THROUGH THOMAS EDISON STATE COLLEGE?
The cost of pursuing a degree through Thomas Edison State College varies, depending on factors such as the number of credits being transferred and the methods used to complete the remaining degree requirements. A student who completes a bachelor's degree within one year may pay $1,500, and one who completes the same degree in two years using different methods may pay $3,000. In short, the more college a student has completed before enrolling, the less that student will pay to complete the desired degree. Students should contact the school to obtain a specific fee schedule.

**HOW CAN YOU OBTAIN MORE INFORMATION
ABOUT THOMAS EDISON STATE COLLEGE?**

To obtain more information about Thomas Edison State College degrees, you can call the Thomas Edison Office of Admissions Services at (609) 292-6565 or write to Thomas Edison State College, 101 West State Street, Trenton, NJ 08608-1176. To obtain more information on the TESC Master of Science in Management degree, you can call (609) 984-1150 or write to Director of Graduate Studies, Master of Science in Management, at the same address. Information on Thomas Edison State College can also be accessed over the Internet at web address: www.tesc.edu.

10

Servicemembers Opportunity Colleges

Servicemembers Opportunity Colleges are colleges and universities that have developed special policies and procedures for military personnel that make it easier for them to earn college degrees. In 1972, these colleges, in cooperation with the Department of Defense, the military services, and one another, formed what is known today as the Servicemembers Opportunity Colleges (SOC) Program. This program is funded by the Department of Defense and is operated through a DANTES contract by the American Association of State Colleges and Universities (AASCU). The SOC Program comprises a network of over 1,000 colleges and universities. The special policies and procedures of these colleges apply only to military students; civilian students must pursue their degrees via the more tedious, more expensive traditional routes. By granting college credit for knowledge gained through nontraditional methods, minimizing the residency requirement, and maximizing the amount of credit allowed for transfer, these schools make it easier for a soldier to earn associate's and bachelor's degrees.

HOW CAN THE SOC PROGRAM HELP YOU?
The SOC Program helps soldiers save money and earn their degrees faster. The transfer practices of SOC Program schools allow soldiers to minimize college credit lost in transfer, thus avoiding duplication of coursework. These schools limit their residency requirements for military personnel to 25 percent of the undergraduate degree program. A school also agrees to accept any course taken at that institution during the SOC agreement period as credit toward the school residency requirement. These policies

help soldiers avoid the need to take extra courses to meet residency requirements. SOC schools have agreed to award college credit for a servicemember's military training and experiences when those credits apply toward the degree being sought. Finally, SOC schools have processes to evaluate and award college credit for nationally recognized extrainstitutional learning such as CLEP Examinations, DSSTs, and ACT-PEPs.

HOW DOES THE SOC PROGRAM WORK?

After seeing an education counselor and selecting an SOC school offering the desired degree, a soldier speaks with a school representative and requests an unofficial evaluation of his or her college work and experiences. To request an evaluation, soldiers must normally have an AARTS transcript or DD Form 295 forwarded to the school. Using the evaluation as a guide, the soldier completes at least 6 semester hours of course work (normally, two classes) toward the selected degree program. The official SOC agreement is then signed by the school and the student. The agreement guarantees that the soldier can earn his or her degree with that institution as long as he or she completes 25 percent of the credits at that school. The remaining degree requirements can be completed at the same college or at any one of the over 1,000 schools that have agreed to abide by the rules of the SOC Program. It does not matter how often a soldier transfers or how many different colleges he or she attends, because the contract is a guarantee. Once the degree requirements are met, the school that signed the SOC agreement awards the degree to the soldier.

HOW MUCH DOES IT COST?

The SOC agreement is free. Of course, all institutions charge their own tuition rates for courses required to complete degree requirements. Be sure to request an evaluation of your college credit and military experiences before taking any classes.

CAN SPOUSES USE THE SOC PROGRAM?

The SOC program was originally designed for servicemembers on active duty in the Army, Navy, and Marine Corps (the Air Force uses the Community College of the Air Force). However, some military education offices help family members get SOC agreements. Many SOC representatives at the colleges will also help. SOC member schools are not bound to honor an agreement with a family member, but they normally do.

ARE SOC SCHOOLS ACCREDITED?

All Servicemember Opportunity Colleges are fully accredited. In order to be a member of the SOC Program, a school must be a degree-granting institution that is accredited by an institutional accrediting agency recognized by the Council on Postsecondary Accreditation.

WHAT KINDS OF DEGREES CAN BE EARNED USING THE SOC PROGRAM?

The full range of associate's, bachelor's, and graduate degrees is awarded by member schools of the SOC Program. Nearly every major imaginable is available through SOC member schools. Soldiers should check with nearby SOC schools to determine the availability of specific degree programs.

WHICH SCHOOLS PARTICIPATE IN THE SOC PROGRAM?

As mentioned earlier, there are over 1,000 member schools of the SOC Program. Following is a small sampling of these schools listed by state. To examine the complete list, make an appointment with your military education counselor and ask to see the *Servicemembers Opportunity Colleges Guide,* which contains over 1,000 pages of valuable information on SOC schools.

Alabama
  Auburn University at Montgomery
  University of Alabama at Birmingham

Alaska
  University of Alaska–Anchorage
  University of Alaska–Fairbanks
  University of Alaska–Southeast

Arizona
  Cochise College
  University of Arizona
  University of Phoenix

Arkansas
  Arkansas State University–Beebe
  Southern Arkansas University
  University of Arkansas at Little Rock

California
  California State University–Bakersfield
  California State University–Hayward
  California State University–Sacramento
  California State University–Stanislaus
  Golden Gate University
  San Diego State University

Colorado
  Colorado State University
  Regis University
  University of Southern Colorado

Connecticut
  Eastern Connecticut State University
  University of Bridgeport
  University of New Haven

Delaware
  Delaware State College
  Goldey-Beacom College
  Wesley College

District of Columbia
  George Washington University
  Southeastern University
  Strayer College
  University of the District of Columbia

Florida
  Saint Leo College
  University of Central Florida
  University of North Florida
  University of South Florida
  University of Tampa
  University of West Florida

Georgia
Armstrong State College
Darton College
Georgia Southern University
Savannah State College

Guam
Guam Community College

Hawaii
Chaminade University of Honolulu
Hawaii Loa College
Hawaii Pacific University

Idaho
Boise State University
College of Southern Idaho
Idaho State University

Illinois
City Colleges of Chicago
Governors State University
Parkland College
Triton College

Indiana
Ball State University
Indiana State University
Marian College
University of Indianapolis

Iowa
Clarke College
Saint Ambrose University
Upper Iowa University

Kansas
Kansas Newman College
University of Kansas
Wichita State University

Kentucky
  Kentucky State University
  Murray State University
  Western Kentucky University

Louisiana
  Louisiana College
  Northwestern State University
  Southeastern Louisiana University

Maine
  Husson College
  Saint Joseph's College
  University of Southern Maine

Maryland
  Bowie State University
  Frostburg State University
  University of Baltimore

Massachusetts
  Fisher College
  Newbury College
  Western New England College

Michigan
  Davenport College of Business
  Northern Michigan University
  Southwestern Michigan College

Minnesota
  Bemidji State University
  Concordia College
  Saint Cloud State University

Mississippi
  Delta State University
  Jackson State University
  Mississippi State University

Missouri
  Lincoln University
  Park College
  Webster University

Montana
  College of Great Falls
  Northern Montana College
  Western Montana College

Nebraska
  Bellevue College
  Nebraska Methodist College of Nursing and Allied Health
  University of Nebraska at Omaha–College of Continuing Studies

Nevada
  University of Nevada–Las Vegas

New Hampshire
  New Hampshire College
  White Pines College

New Jersey
  Bloomfield College
  Saint Peter's College
  Thomas A. Edison State College

New Mexico
  College of Santa Fe
  Eastern New Mexico University
  San Juan College

New York
  Pace University
  Regents College, University of the State of New York
  Saint Thomas Aquinas College
  State University of New York at Buffalo

North Carolina
  Campbell University
  North Carolina State University
  Wingate College

North Dakota
Minot State University
University of North Dakota–Grand Forks
University of North Dakota–Lake Region

Ohio
Franklin University
Ohio State University
University of Akron

Oklahoma
Oklahoma State University
Rogers State College
University of Central Oklahoma

Oregon
Eastern Oregon State College
George Fox College
Western Oregon State College

Pennsylvania
Berean Institute
Pennsylvania State University at Harrisburg
Temple University
Wilson College

Puerto Rico
Inter American University of Puerto Rico

Rhode Island
Rhode Island College
Salve Regina College

South Carolina
Charleston Southern University
Newberry College
University of South Carolina

South Dakota
Black Hills State University
Huron University
South Dakota State University

Tennessee
Austin Peay State University
East Tennessee State University
Middle Tennessee State University

Texas
Incarnate Word College
Saint Mary's University
University of Central Texas
University of Mary Hardin–Baylor

Utah
College of Eastern Utah
Weber State University

Vermont
Southern Vermont College
Trinity College

Virginia
Averett College
Hampton University
Norfolk State University
Old Dominion University

Washington
City University
Eastern Washington University
Pierce College

West Virginia
Bluefield State College
West Virginia University

Wisconsin
  Silver Lake College
  University of Wisconsin–Superior
  University of Wisconsin–Whitewater

Wyoming
  Eastern Wyoming College

11

Educational Programs and Benefits

This chapter covers educational counseling and career planning, information about the Montgomery GI Bill and financial assistance for college expenses, high school completion services, college admissions tests, assistance in becoming a teacher, Army correspondence courses, and information about unique nontraditional educational opportunities. These are all available through the Army Education Center (AEC), which is your education headquarters.

ARE THE SAME SERVICES AVAILABLE AT THE AIR FORCE AND NAVY EDUCATION CENTERS?
The education center, regardless of whether it is an Army, Navy, Air Force, or Marine Education Center, provides the same valuable programs. Of course, resources vary not only among services, but also among installations. As a general rule, however, education counselors provide the same services to military personnel, regardless of service affiliation. Generally, the only prerequisite for using those services is that you must be assigned to that particular post or base.

WHAT TYPE OF CAREER PLANNING DOES THE AEC OFFER?
The AEC offers many different types of career planning using many unique programs and systems, such as the DANTES Computer Assisted Guidance Information Systems (CAGIS), the Campbell Interest and Skill Survey (CISS), the Career Assessment Inventory (CAI) Enhanced Version, the Career Planning Program (CPP), the Holland Self-Directed Search (SDS), the Kuder Occupational Interest Survey, the Strong Interest Inventory (SII), the Test of Adult Basic Education (TABE), and the Myers-Briggs Type Indicator (MBTI).

WHAT EXACTLY ARE THESE
CAREER PLANNING PROGRAMS AND SYSTEMS?

CAGIS is a collection of DANTES interactive computer-assisted guidance and career planning information systems. CAGIS allows individuals to use personal information to interact with the computer and reach more reasonable decisions regarding educational and vocational choices. Currently, there are two systems being used as part of CAGIS: DISCOVER and the Guidance Information System (GIS). DISCOVER is used to assess interests, abilities, and values and provide information on related occupations and educational opportunities. GIS is used to locate facts about colleges, professional schools, occupations, military careers, and financial aid.

CISS is a modern survey that measures self-interests and skills. It is used to help counselors obtain more complete career assessment information. This survey provides both an interest scale and a confidence scale. The interest scale reflects the individual's degree of attraction for a specified occupational area. The confidence scale is a parallel skills scale that provides an estimate of the individual's confidence in his or her ability to perform various occupational activities. Together, these scales provide more comprehensive and valuable data than interest scores alone. CISS focuses on careers that require some degree of college education and is most appropriate for individuals who are college bound.

CAI helps counselors and soldiers make career decisions by measuring interests requiring a minimum of postsecondary education, such as community college, technical, or business school training. CAI contains basic interest scales that provide specific information about a person's interests in twenty-five different career areas, such as electronics and medical service occupations. CAI also has occupational scales that relate to 111 specific careers and indicate the interest areas that an individual has in common with workers who are successfully employed in that particular field.

CPP is a program consisting of an ability test battery, an interest inventory, scales for assessing career-related experiences, and a background and plans inventory. Examinees receive a comprehensive two-page score report that integrates results from these components and relates them to the World-of-Work Map.

SDS is an interest test that allows soldiers to find the occupations that best suit their interests and skills. The format is easy to use, and the test can be taken, scored, and interpreted by the individual without assistance. SDS contains an occupational finder that contains over 1,300 occupational possibilities.

The Kuder Occupational Interest Survey suggests promising occupations and college majors in rank order, based on the individual's pattern. The occupations range from those requiring professional schooling to those requiring technical school training. The Kuder is one of the oldest interest surveys on the market today.

SII is an inventory that measures a person's interest in careers requiring advanced technical or college training. Basic interest scales provide specific information about a person's interests in twenty-three career fields, such as medical science, law/politics, and business management. Occupational scales relate to 111 specific careers and indicate areas of career satisfaction. The Strong on-line software was updated in 1994 from a DOS version to a Windows version to simplify administration.

TABE measures the application of basic skills: reading, vocabulary, reading comprehension, mathematics computation, mathematics concepts and applications, language mechanics, language expression, and spelling. Completion of TABE is a prerequisite for attendance at NCO Education System (NCOES) schools.

MBTI is designed to help individuals understand their strengths and evaluate their differences and similarities. It outlines basic differences in perception and judgment. Perception uses sensing and intuition to evaluate the paths to awareness of things, people, happenings, or ideas. Judgment uses thinking and feeling to evaluate all the ways of coming to conclusions about what has been perceived.

WHAT IS THE MONTGOMERY GI BILL?
The Montgomery GI Bill is a program of educational benefits for military personnel.

HOW MUCH DOES THE MONTGOMERY GI BILL PAY FOR EDUCATIONAL BENEFITS?
Veterans who served on active duty for three years or more, or who served two years on active duty plus four years in the Selected Reserve or National Guard, can receive thirty-six monthly payments of $416.62.

WHO IS ELIGIBLE TO RECEIVE BENEFITS UNDER THE MONTGOMERY GI BILL?
Individuals who entered active duty for the first time after June 30, 1985, and received an honorable discharge are eligible for the Montgomery GI Bill. Active duty includes full-time National Guard duty performed after

November 29, 1989. To receive the maximum benefit, participants must serve continuously for three years. Individuals may also qualify for the full benefit by serving two continuous years on active duty, followed by four years of Selected Reserve service beginning within one year of release from active duty. Participants must meet the requirement for a high school diploma or an equivalency certificate before the first period of active duty ends. Completing 12 credit hours toward a college degree meets this requirement. Individuals who serve at least three years of continuous active duty, even though they were obligated to serve less, will be paid the maximum benefit.

For the most part, benefits under the Montgomery GI Bill end ten years from the date of the veteran's last discharge or release from active duty. The Veterans Administration can extend this ten-year period if the veteran was prevented from training during this period because of a disability or because he or she was held by a foreign government or power. The ten-year period can also be extended if an individual reenters active duty for ninety days or more after becoming eligible. Veterans serving periods of active duty of less than ninety days can qualify for extensions under certain circumstances. If the veteran's discharge is upgraded by the military, the ten-year period begins on the date of the upgrade. If eligibility is based on both the Vietnam Era GI Bill and the Montgomery GI Bill and discharge from active duty was before December 31, 1989, the veteran will have until January 1, 2000, to collect benefits. The Veterans Administration subtracts from the ten-year period those periods during which the veteran was not on active duty between January 1, 1977, and June 30, 1985. If eligibility is based on two years of active duty and four years in the Selected Reserve, the veteran's eligibility will end ten years from his or her release from active duty or ten years from completion of the four-year Selected Reserve obligation, whichever is later.

HOW DO YOU ENROLL
IN THE MONTGOMERY GI BILL PROGRAM?

Servicemembers normally enroll in the Montgomery GI Bill Program upon entry into the military. To participate in the Montgomery GI Bill, servicemembers must have their military pay reduced by $100 a month for the first twelve months of active duty. This servicemember contribution to the program is mandatory, and the money is not refundable. If an individual decides not to participate in the program, that decision cannot be changed at a later date, except in special circumstances. An exception is made for servicemembers who are involuntarily separated from active duty with an honorable discharge. A second exception is made for those who voluntarily separate from active duty under force reduction programs.

FOR WHAT TYPES OF EDUCATION OR TRAINING CAN THE MONTGOMERY GI BILL BE USED?

The Montgomery Gl Bill can be used to pay for:

1. Courses at colleges and universities leading to associate's, bachelor's, or graduate degrees and accredited independent study. Cooperative training programs are available to individuals not on active duty.

2. Courses leading to a certificate or diploma from a business, technical, or vocational school.

3. Apprenticeship or on-the-job training programs for individuals not on active duty.

4. Correspondence courses, under certain conditions.

5. Flight training. Before beginning training, the veteran must have a private pilot's license and meet the physical requirements for a commercial license. Benefits also may be received for flying hours up to the minimum required by the Federal Aviation Administration for the rating or certification being pursued.

6. Tutorial assistance benefits if the individual is enrolled in school half-time or more. Remedial, deficiency, and refresher training also may be available.

WHAT OTHER KINDS OF FINANCIAL ASSISTANCE CAN YOU OBTAIN FROM THE AEC?

Financial assistance for college comes in many forms. The experts at the AEC can provide valuable information and counseling about all types of financial assistance for college education, including educational grants, scholarships, work-study, and loans. In addition to information about student aid offered by the federal and state governments, the AEC maintains information about financial assistance offered by private companies, labor unions, business organizations, foundations, religious organizations, fraternities and sororities, town and city clubs, and community and civic groups such as the American Legion, YMCA, 4-H Club, Elks, Kiwanis, Jaycees, and Girl and Boy Scouts. The AEC also provides the Application for Federal Student Aid Form, which is the first step to obtaining student financial aid such as Federal Pell Grants, Federal Stafford Loans, Federal PLUS Loans, Federal Consolidation Loans, Federal Supplemental Educational Opportunity Grants, Federal Work-Study, and Federal Perkins Loans. The latest information on military tuition assistance funding and limitations is also available at the AEC.

HOW CAN THE AEC HELP A SOLDIER FINISH HIGH SCHOOL?
The AEC can help soldiers receive high school equivalency diplomas through the General Educational Development (GED) Test. The GED is designed specifically for those adults who never completed high school. It is composed of a battery of five tests (writing skills, social studies, interpreting literature and the arts, science, and mathematics) designed to measure the general skills and knowledge usually acquired in four years of high school study. These tests were developed by the GED Testing Service according to specifications established by professional educators in each subject area. Soldiers can earn the equivalent of a high school diploma by passing all five parts of the GED. Each year, hundreds of military personnel earn high school equivalency diplomas by passing the GED.

WHICH COLLEGE ADMISSIONS TESTS
ARE OFFERED BY THE AEC?
The AEC administers many different college admissions tests, including the American College Testing (ACT) Assessment Program, the Scholastic Assessment Test (SAT), the Graduate Management Admission Test (GMAT), the Praxis Series Teachers Examinations, and the Law School Admission Test (LSAT).

WHAT ARE THESE COLLEGE ADMISSIONS TESTS?
ACT is a program that assesses general educational development and measures the performance of intellectual tasks required by a college student. The examination consists of English, mathematics, reading, and science reasoning.

The SAT measures verbal and mathematical abilities. The verbal portions include vocabulary, verbal reasoning, and reading comprehension. The mathematical portions test mathematical reasoning using arithmetic, algebra, and geometry and emphasize problem-solving aptitude rather than advanced achievement in mathematics.

The GMAT measures general verbal and quantitative abilities, developed over a long period of time, that are associated with success in the first year of study at a graduate school of management.

Praxis is actually three separate tests that measure communication skills, general knowledge, and professional knowledge. The Praxis Specialty Area Tests measure understanding of the content and methods applicable to the specific subject area. The LSAT is designed to assist law schools in assessing the academic potential of their applicants. It measures skills that are considered essential for success in law school, such as the ability to process information to reach conclusions. The LSAT is not funded by DANTES.

HOW CAN THE AEC HELP YOU BECOME A TEACHER?

In addition to many other services, the AEC offers programs designed to assist soldiers in their transition into the civilian world. One such program, the Troops to Teachers (TTT) Program, has helped many soldiers become qualified teachers. The primary goal of TTT is to place math and science teachers, but it places qualified teachers in any subject. About 25 percent of the personnel placed through TTT have been placed in math or science, 16 percent in the elementary grades, 15 percent in special education or working with at-risk students, 10 percent in English and social studies, 6 percent in vocational education, and the remainder in subjects from art and music to bilingual education. The greatest need for teachers is in rural and inner-city school districts. TTT participants have proved to be strong, positive role models, and they are especially attractive to school districts serving a large percentage of students from one-parent families. TTT participants are valued for their strong academic backgrounds, leadership skills, personal confidence, maturity, and professionalism and have a reputation as excellent and highly effective teachers. The referral and placement assistance process includes guidance and counseling on alternative certification programs, certification requirements, and identification of potential employment opportunities. The most important part of this process is referral. Individuals in the TTT database are referred to school districts requesting lists of TTT participants who are interested in teaching in their states. Additionally, information is provided to participants regarding teacher shortages reported by school districts. Those soldiers interested in becoming teachers should contact their AECs about submitting applications for TTT through DANTES.

CAN YOU GET COLLEGE CREDIT
FOR ARMY CORRESPONDENCE COURSES?

Army correspondence courses are an important element in professional development and in getting promoted. As a general rule, college credit is not awarded for Army correspondence courses. There are only a few courses available in the Department of the Army (DA) Pamphlet 351-20, *Army Correspondence Course Program Catalog*, that are recommended by the American Council on Education (ACE) for college credit. These courses are generally not available to most soldiers. In addition, it does not appear likely that the ACE will evaluate or recommend credit for any other courses in the near future. If you are interested in pursuing Army correspondence courses for professional development, ask your ESO for DA Form 145, Army Correspondence Course Enrollment Application, and review DA Pamphlet 351-20 to decide on a course that interests you.

WHAT ARE SOME OTHER SOURCES OF COLLEGE CREDIT?

Some colleges and universities may grant college credit to soldiers for national and professional certifications, Air Force extension courses, Air Force-instructed military courses or training, Defense Language Institute (DLI) courses, Defense Language Proficiency Tests (DLPTs), and Internet and on-line courses.

WHAT ARE NATIONAL CERTIFICATION TESTS?

National Certification Tests are designed to allow an individual to demonstrate a specified degree of knowledge and skill required to earn certification as a professional in a particular field. National certifications are used in the civilian community to establish a common level of expertise within certain career fields. Soldiers who pass National Certification Tests are recognized alongside their civilian counterparts as professionals in their respective fields.

HOW CAN YOU GET COLLEGE CREDIT
FOR TAKING A NATIONAL CERTIFICATION TEST?

In addition to providing professional credentials that are easily recognizable to civilians, these tests are used by some nontraditional institutions, such as Regents College, as the basis for awarding college credit for life and work experience. DANTES has agreements with many professional agencies that allow their examinations to be administered at military education centers worldwide. Make an appointment to talk with your ESO about when you can take these tests.

HOW MUCH DO NATIONAL CERTIFICATION TESTS COST?

Costs vary. It is best to speak with an ESO before deciding to take a certification test, since test dates and availability also vary.

WHAT ARE THE DIFFERENT TYPES
OF NATIONAL CERTIFICATION TESTS OFFERED?

Many of the National Certification Tests are listed below:

Association of Boards of Certification-Uniform Program for Reciprocity (ABC)

American Board of Industrial Hygiene (ABIH) Board of Certified Safety Professionals (BCSP) Joint Committee for Certification of Occupational Health and Safety Technicians

American Council on Exercise (ACE)

Accredited Financial Counselor (AFC) Program

American Medical Technologist (AMT)

American Nurses Credentialing Center (ANCC)

National Institute for Automotive Service Excellence (ASE)

American Speech-Language-Hearing Association (ASHA)

Association of State and Provincial Psychology Boards (ASPPB)

American Society for Quality Control (ASQC)

Board of Certified Safety Professionals (BCSP)

Certified Board of General Dentistry (CBGD)

Cardiovascular Credentialing International (CCI)

Dental Assisting National Board (DANB)

National Registry of Emergency Medical Technicians (EMT)

Electronics Technicians Association, International (ETA-I)

Food Protection Certification Program (FPCP)

Institute for Certification of Computing Professionals (ICCP)

Institute of Certified Professional Managers (ICPM)

Credentialing Commission of the International Society for Clinical Laboratory Technology (ISCLT)

Liaison Council on Certification for the Surgical Technologist (LCC-ST)

National Association of Radio and Telecommunications Engineers, Inc. (NARTE)

National Association of Social Workers (NASW)

National Board for the Certification of Orthopaedic Technologists (NBCOT)

National Board of Respiratory Care (NBRC)

National Institute for Certification in Engineering Technology (NICET)

National Institute for the Certification of Healthcare Sterile Processing and Distribution Personnel (NICHSPDP)

Professional Secretaries International (PSI)

Society of Broadcast Engineers (SBE)

WHAT ARE AIR FORCE EXTENSION COURSES?
Air Force extension courses are correspondence courses offered through the U.S. Air Force Extension Course Institute (ECI), which provides voluntary, nonresident, career-broadening courses to military and civilian personnel in the Department of Defense. The ECI offers nearly 300 courses in career fields ranging from Aircrew Operations to Security Police.

ARE THESE COURSES RECOMMENDED FOR COLLEGE CREDIT?
The Air Force attempts to have all ECI courses continually evaluated by ACE and accredited through the National Home Study Council. For these reasons, most, but not all, ECI courses, are recommended for college credit.

IS THERE A CHARGE FOR ECI COURSES?
The prices for ECI courses vary from approximately $1 to $30 for Department of Defense personnel. The average cost of ECI courses for military personnel is approximately $15. Prices are higher for nonmilitary personnel.

CAN ARMY PERSONNEL ENROLL IN THESE COURSES?
Army personnel are eligible to enroll in nearly all ECI courses.

HOW DO YOU ENROLL IN AN ECI COURSE?
Soldiers who desire to enroll in an ECI course should see their ESO and ask to see the *USAF Extension Course Institute Catalog* and price listing. After deciding on a course, the soldier completes ECI Form 23, and the ESO signs it and submits it, along with a cashier's check or money order (provided by the soldier) for the exact amount of the course.

HOW CAN YOU GET COLLEGE CREDIT FOR AIR FORCE–INSTRUCTED MILITARY COURSES OR TRAINING?
Many of the official courses and training taught under the authority of the Air Force are affiliated with the Community College of the Air Force (CCAF), which awards college credit for many military training experiences. Many of these Air Force courses are offered to personnel of the other services, including the Army. If you are not sure whether an Air Force-taught course you attended is eligible for credit, request a transcript from the CCAF.

HOW DO YOU REQUEST A TRANSCRIPT FROM THE CCAF?

Soldiers who have completed an Air Force course may request a transcript from the CCAF by completing Air Force (AF) Form 2099, Request for Community College of the Air Force Transcript. These forms are available at most military education centers. If you do not have AF Form 2099, you can write to the CCAF directly at Registrar, CCAF/RR, Maxwell AFB, AL 36112. In that correspondence, include your full name; social security number; pay grade; and the number, title, location, and dates of the course or courses taken through the Air Force.

HOW MUCH DOES A TRANSCRIPT FROM THE CCAF COST?

The transcript is free.

IS THE CCAF ACCREDITED?

The CCAF is fully accredited by the Southern Association of Colleges and Schools.

CAN ARMY PERSONNEL ENROLL IN THE CCAF?

Although Army personnel may take some individual courses granted credit by the CCAF and may request a transcript, only enlisted members of the Air Force may enroll in a degree program.

WHAT ARE DEFENSE LANGUAGE INSTITUTE (DLI) COURSES?

The Presidio of Monterey, California, teaches a variety of foreign languages to military and U.S. government personnel. Languages taught at the DLI include modern European Languages, Arabic, Japanese, Russian, and Tagalog.

ARE DLI COURSES RECOMMENDED FOR COLLEGE CREDIT?

All DLI courses have been evaluated by ACE and are recommended for varying amounts of college credit. The courses at DLI normally last between six and eighteen months. Longer courses are generally recommended for more college credit than shorter courses. Even the short courses, however, can be valuable sources of college credit. For example, the basic Spanish course lasts six months (twenty-five weeks) and is recommended by ACE for 12 semester hours of college credit in the following categories: 3 semester hours in Spanish Elements I, 3 semester hours in Spanish Elements II, 3 semester hours in Spanish Composition and Culture, and 3 semester hours in Spanish Readings.

HOW CAN YOU GET A TRANSCRIPT FROM THE DLI?

Soldiers who have completed a course at the DLI may request a transcript by sending a written request to DLI/FLC, Academic Records Division, Presidio of Monterey, CA 93944-5006. Include your full name, social security number, course number (if known), course name, dates of attendance, and the address where you would like the transcript sent.

HOW MUCH DOES A DLI TRANSCRIPT COST?

The transcript is free.

IS THE DLI ACCREDITED?

The DLI is accredited by the Accrediting Commission for Community and Junior Colleges of the Western Association of Schools and Colleges.

CAN ARMY PERSONNEL ENROLL AT THE DLI?

The DLI is open to all Army personnel. Selection for attendance at the DLI is dependent on MOS requirements, Defense Language Aptitude Battery scores, and the needs of the Army. Soldiers interested in attending the DLI should see their unit career counselors.

WHAT ARE DEFENSE LANGUAGE PROFICIENCY TESTS (DLPTS)?

DLPTs measure the ability to speak, read, and understand a language. The DLPT is related to the Defense Language Institute, but only in some ways. When students complete language courses at the DLI, they are required to take the DLPT to measure their speaking, listening, and reading abilities. The DLPT is also used as the basis for awarding foreign language proficiency pay (FLPP) to soldiers in select fields.

HOW CAN YOU GET COLLEGE CREDIT FOR A DLPT?

Some nontraditional schools, such as Regents College, award college credit for certain scores on the DLPT. There is an important distinction between DLI courses and the DLPT. Basic courses completed at the DLI are normally recommended only for lower-level bachelor's degree credit. Certain scores on the DLPT result in recommended college credit in both the upper and the lower divisions. The DLPT can be a valuable source of upper-level college credit for soldiers seeking a bachelor's degree. Much of the credit awarded on the DLPT is in addition to any credit already received from DLI courses. All DLPT scores are annotated on DA Form 330, Language Proficiency Questionnaire, and signed by the reporting officer (normally the test proctor). For the purposes of awarding college credit, most schools require a certified copy of the DLPT.

HOW CAN YOU GET A CERTIFIED COPY
OF YOUR DLPT RESULTS?

A certified copy may be obtained from the Test Control Officer who normally administers the DLPT in your area or from your ESO. In some cases, a MILPO official may agree to certify a copy of your DLPT results, as long as an original copy is on file in your personnel records. If you need a certified copy of a DLPT taken at the DLI, you may request in writing that a certified copy be sent to you or to the school you are attending. All requests for DLPTs should be sent to DLI/FLC, Attn: EST, DLPT Score Reports, Presidio of Monterey, CA 93944-5006. Be sure to include your full name, social security number, the language tested, the date you took the DLPT, and the address of the school where you want the copy sent. Request that the DLPT copy be certified. Most schools do not accept DLPT copies, certified or not, that are mailed by the student; the certifying official must mail the DLPT for you.

DOES IT COST ANYTHING TO TAKE THE DLPT?
The DLPT is free.

ARE DLI GRADUATES THE ONLY ONES
WHO CAN TAKE A DLPT?
The DLPT is not restricted to DLI graduates. Anyone who believes that he or she has proficiency in a foreign language may request to take a DLPT. This does not mean that everyone who requests to take the DLPT is allowed to do so. Factors that are considered when approving a request to take a DLPT are the commander's recommendation, the justification for taking the test, MOS requirements, and the Army's need for the language. Army AECs require that the soldier submit a DA Form 4187, Personnel Action, requesting the DLPT. Also, it is important to note that only those personnel in select MOSs are awarded FLPP.

WHAT ABOUT INTERNET AND ON-LINE COURSES?
Anyone who uses one of the popular on-line computer services is probably aware that many colleges and universities offer courses over the World Wide Web (WWW). Some of these schools even offer degrees that can be earned by computer. Despite the easy access of the programs, however, most of the courses offered are expensive; a single course might cost over

$1,000. Many soldiers are attracted by the convenience of these courses. Others see the computer as yet another nontraditional route for pursuing a degree. If some of these courses interest you, it is advisable to check with the AEC to determine whether the school is actually accredited by a recognized accrediting agency (see Appendix C). Although it is not possible to offer a complete list, the following list includes many of the schools presently providing courses over the WWW:

Aalborg University
Acadia University
Arizona State University
Australian National University
Bilkent University
Boston University
Bridgewater College
Brigham Young University
Brown University
Bucknell University
Butler University
California Institute of Technology
California Polytechnic State University
Carnegie Mellon University
Case Western Reserve University
Colorado State University
Columbia University
Cornell University
Dalhousie University
Dartmouth College
Davenport University
Dixie College
Duke University
Embry-Riddle Aeronautical University
Emory University
Five College Marine Sciences
Geneva University
Georgetown University
Georgia Institute of Technology
Gustavus Adolphus College
Halmstad University
Hamline University
Hanover College

Harvard University
Harvey Mudd College
Honolulu Community College
Indiana University
Iowa State University
Jacksonville State University
James Cook University
Johns Hopkins University
Kansas State University
Linkoping University
Louisiana Tech University
Loyola College
Ludwig Maximilians University (Munich)
Luther College
Massachusetts Institute of Technology
Michigan State University
Mississippi State University
Mount Saint Mary's College
New Jersey Institute of Technology
New Mexico Tech
New York University
North Carolina State University
Northeastern University
Northwestern University
Oakland University
Ohio State University
Oklahoma State University
Oxford University
Pennsylvania State University
Plymouth State College
Pomona College
Princeton University
Purdue University
Quincey University
Rice University
Richland College
Rogaland University Center
Rutgers University
Saint Joseph's College
Saint Olaf College

San Diego State University
San Francisco State University
Stanford University
State University of West Georgia
Stockholm University
SUNY Institute of Technology
Syracuse University
Technical University of Munich
Technical University of Nova Scotia
Texas A&M University
Trenton State College
Trinity College
Tufts University
Tulane University
University of Alabama
University of Alaska
University of Arizona
University of Arkansas
University of Bath
University of British Columbia
University of California at Berkeley
University of California at Davis
University of California at Irvine
University of California at Los Angeles
University of California at Riverside
University of California at San Diego
University of California at San Francisco
University of California at Santa Barbara
University of California at Santa Cruz
University of Cambridge
University of Colorado at Boulder
University of Colorado at Colorado Springs
University of Colorado at Denver
University of Delaware
University of Edinburgh
University of Hannover
University of Hawaii
University of Houston
University of Idaho
University of Iowa

University of Kansas
University of Limerick
University of Manchester
University of Manitoba
University of Massachusetts–Amherst
University of Massachusetts–Boston
University of Massachusetts–Dartmouth
University of Massachusetts–Lowell
University of Massachusetts–Worcester
University of Miami
University of Michigan
University of Mississippi
University of Nevada–Las Vegas
University of New Brunswick
University of North Carolina
University of North Carolina at Charlotte
University of Notre Dame
University of Nottingham
University of Oklahoma
University of Oregon
University of Ottawa
University of Pennsylvania
University of Pisa
University of Pittsburgh
University of Rochester
University of San Diego
University of Sheffield
University of Southern California
University of Texas at Austin
University of Texas at Dallas
University of Toronto
University of Utah
University of Vermont
University of Virginia
University of Washington
University of Waterloo
University of Wisconsin at Milwaukee
Utah State University
Virginia Tech
Wake Forest University

Warsaw University of Technology
Washington University in St. Louis
Willamette University
Worcester Polytechnic Institute
Yale University
York College of Pennsylvania
Youngstown State University

12

Final Tips

Remember that education involves willpower and discipline as much as it does intellect. Getting started is often a large part of the battle, and by reading this book, you have already begun your educational journey. By now you should feel more comfortable, more optimistic, and less ignorant about your opportunities to pursue a college education.

The following study and test taking tips offer some practical advice. These tips have been gleaned from years of experience and tempered by both success and failure. They have already proved effective for many soldiers pursuing a college education. Use them, and your journey will be an easier one.

STUDY TIPS

1. Study in a location that is free from distractions. If you need background noise to concentrate, it is better to use the radio than the television. But be sure to tune to a classical station so that you won't be tempted to sing along with the music. Classical music also has a calming effect that facilitates concentration.

2. Develop a study routine by studying in the same place daily. Studying daily for short periods works much better than cramming the night before a test.

3. Reward yourself for positive study habits by saving dessert, rental movies, and enjoyable hobbies until after you have completed your daily studying. Be sure that your studying is focused on learning or mastering a particular concept or quantitative amount of knowledge rather than on the amount of time spent studying. In other words, focus on learning objectives rather than on studying for a set amount of time.

4. Kill two birds with one stone by studying while you exercise. Treadmills and exercise bicycles allow for simultaneous reading and exer-

cise. Public libraries and book stores often have books on cassette that can be used in a portable cassette player during exercise.

5. Review material as much as practical within the first twenty-four hours after studying. Most forgetting occurs during this period, so reinforcement and repetition are fundamental. By reviewing regularly, your retention of studied material will improve markedly.

TEST TAKING TIPS

1. Learn as much as possible about a test before you take it. Ask your ESO for any bulletins, sample tests, or flyers available on the test you will be taking. Learn what is expected, the exact type of test to be given, its format, what knowledge is being tested, and how the tests are scored. Knowing as much as possible about the test in advance will relieve stress and help you feel more comfortable during the test.

2. Prepare as much as possible. Take advantage of the sample tests offered by your education center, and practice taking the sample tests under timed conditions. Review any questions that you may have missed. Pay particular attention to the directions for each question missed. Many questions are answered incorrectly because the directions were not fully understood or not fully read.

3. Be mentally and physically alert. Get plenty of sleep the night before the test. Depart for the test site early as a precaution against unexpected delays, such as traffic. Take your identification and several extra No. 2 pencils. Dress comfortably. Select a seat in the testing room away from potential distractions. Do not sit next to your friends.

4. On mathematical questions, do not waste time completing long computations unless the question asks for a specific answer. If an approximate answer is required, you may eliminate the incorrect answers before finishing long computations.

Helping soldiers in their quest for a college education is the goal of this book. I hope that this goal has been accomplished by informing and educating you about the many nontraditional opportunities for pursuing a college education. Good luck.

PART III

APPENDIXES

Appendix A

Abbreviations

AA	Associate in Arts degree
AARTS	Army/ACE Registry Transcript System
AASCU	American Association of State Colleges and Universities
ACAP	Army Career and Alumni Program
ACCP	Army Correspondence Course Program
ACE	American Council on Education
ACES	Army Continuing Education System
ACF	Army College Fund
ACT	American College Testing
ACT-PEP	American College Testing Proficiency Examination Program
AEC	Army Education Center
AIPD	Army Institute for Professional Development
AIT	Advanced Individual Training
ANCOC	Advanced Noncommissioned Officer Course
ANX	abbreviation for Annex
AP	Advanced Placement
APFT	Army Physical Fitness Test
AS	Associate in Science degree
ASVAB	Armed Services Vocational Aptitude Battery
BA	Bachelor of Arts degree
BDFS	Bachelor's Degree for Soldiers
BNCOC	Basic Noncommissioned Officer Course
BS	Bachelor in Science Degree
CAGIS	DANTES Computer Assisted Guidance Information Systems
CAI	Career Assessment Inventory
CCAF	Community College of the Air Force

CCE	Course Credit by Examination (Ohio University)
CISS	Campbell Interest and Skill Survey
CLEP	College Level Examination Program
CML	Commercial
CONUS	Continental United States
CPP	Career Planning Program
DANTES	Defense Activity for Non-Traditional Education Support
DETC	Distance Education and Training Council
DLI	Defense Language Institute
DLI/FLC	Defense Language Institute/Foreign Language Center
DLPT	Defense Language Proficiency Test
DOE	Department of Education
DSN	Defense Switching Network
DSST	DANTES Subject Standardized Test
ECI	Air Force Extension Course Institute
ESO	Education Services Officer
ETS	Educational Testing Service
FLPP	foreign language proficiency pay
GED	General Educational Development
GMAT	Graduate Management Admission Test
GPA	grade point average
GRE	Graduate Record Examination
GT	General Technical
LSAT	Law School Admission Test
MA	Master of Arts degree
MBTI	Myers-Briggs Type Indicator
MEU	Mind Extension University
MILPO	Military Personnel Office
MOS	Military Occupational Specialty
MS	Master of Science degree
NCO	noncommissioned officer
NCOES	NCO Education System
OCONUS	Outside the Continental United States
OCS	Officer Candidate School
OSB	Officer Selection Battery
PLDC	Primary Leadership Development Course
PONSI	Program on Noncollegiate Sponsored Instruction
QH	quarter hour
RCE	Regents College Exam

SAT	Scholastic Assessment Test
SDS	Holland Self-Directed Search
SH	semester hour
SII	Strong Interest Inventory
SOC	Servicemembers Opportunity College
SOCAD	SOC Army Degrees
SOCAD-2	SOC Army Degrees (associate's degree)
SOCAD-4	SOC Army Degrees (bachelor's degree)
SOCBDFS	SOC Bachelor's Degree for Soldiers (now known as SOCAD-4)
SOCNAV-2	SOC Navy (associate's degree)
SOCNAV-4	SOC Navy (bachelor's degree)
SOCMAR-2	SOC Marine Corps (associate's degree)
SOCMAR-4	SOC Marine Corps (bachelor's degree)
TA	tuition assistance
TABE	Test of Adult Basic Education
TCO	Test Control Officer
TECEP	Thomas Edison College Examination Program
TESC	Thomas Edison State College
TTT	Troops to Teachers
USAFI	United States Air Force Institute
WWW	World Wide Web

Appendix B

Definitions

Associate's Degree A degree that normally requires completion of at least two but less than four years of full-time equivalent college-level work (usually 60 semester hours).

Bachelor's Degree A degree that normally requires completion of four but no more than five years of full-time equivalent college-level work (usually 120 semester hours).

Doctor's Degree A degree that normally requires completion of a program of study beyond the master's degree. It is the highest degree that can be awarded for graduate study. These degrees include the Doctor of Philosophy (Ph.D.) and the Doctor of Education (Ed.D.).

First-Professional Degree A degree that requires completion of a program that includes at least two years of college work before entering the program, completion of the academic requirements to begin practice in the profession, and a total of at least six academic years of college work to complete the degree program, including prior required college work plus the length of the professional program itself. These degrees include the first-professional degree in law (J.D.) or the first-professional degree in medicine (M.D.).

Master's Degree A degree that normally requires completion of a program of study, consisting of the full-time equivalent of one to two academic years of work beyond the bachelor's degree.

Quarter A unit of time in an academic calendar. The quarter system is used less often than the semester system. Colleges using the quarter system normally divide the school year into three quarters, with the first quarter lasting from September to December, the second quarter from January to March, and the third quarter from March to May. The fourth quarter constitutes summer vacation.

Quarter Hour A unit of college credit used to represent completion of a subject normally pursued for approximately one hour per week during the quarter. This unit of college credit is used less often than the semester hour. Most colleges using the quarter system offer classes in units of 3 quarter hours. A class worth 3 quarter hours, for example, would meet for a total of approximately 3 hours during each week of the quarter.

Semester The most common unit of time in an academic calendar. Normally, a school year is divided into two semesters, with the first semester lasting from August to December, and the second semester from January to May.

Semester Hour A unit of college credit used to represent completion of a subject normally pursued for approximately one hour per week during the semester. This is the most common unit of college credit. Most college classes are offered in units of 3 semester hours, although classes worth more or less credit are not uncommon. A class worth 3 semester hours would meet for a total of approximately 3 hours during each week of the semester.

Appendix C

Accreditation and Accrediting Agencies

WHAT IS ACCREDITATION?
Accreditation means that a school has been evaluated and approved by an accrediting agency or association found by the U.S. Department of Education to be a reliable authority on the quality of education offered by educational institutions or programs. The Department of Education categorizes accrediting agencies and associations as either regional institutional accrediting associations or national institutional and specialized accrediting agencies.

IS ACCREDITATION IMPORTANT?
Accreditation is very important, because if you attend a school that is not accredited by a U.S. accrediting agency, you may be wasting both your time and your money. Many employers, both civilian and government, do not recognize degrees granted by institutions that are not accredited by an agency or association approved by the U.S. Department of Education. This also means that many accredited schools do not accept college credit transferred from nonaccredited schools. An institution must be accredited before most federal and private financial assistance can be granted.

**IF A SCHOOL SAYS THAT IT IS ACCREDITED,
CAN YOU BELIEVE IT?**
You cannot always believe what you read in a college brochure or catalog. Many schools claim that they are accredited by this or that world organization or agency. There are many accrediting organizations that are not recognized by the U.S. Department of Education as being reliable authorities on the quality of education. Many of these organizations have poor

reputations, and their approval or "accreditation" of a school means little. Before enrolling in a school, make sure that it is accredited by an agency or organization approved by the U.S. Department of Education.

HOW DO YOU VERIFY THAT A SCHOOL IS ACTUALLY ACCREDITED?

Soldiers planning to enroll at an institution should contact the accrediting agency to verify that the school is accredited. All regional institutional accrediting associations and national institutional and specialized accrediting agencies recognized by the U.S. Department of Education are listed below:

Regional Institutional Accrediting Associations

Middle States Association of Colleges and Schools Commission
   on Higher Education and Commission on Secondary Schools
3624 Market Street
Philadelphia, PA 19104
(215) 662-5606

New England Association of Schools and Colleges Sanborn House
15 High Street
Winchester, MA 01891
(617) 729-6762

North Central Association of Colleges and Schools Commission
   on Institutions of Higher Education
159 North Dearborn Street
Chicago, IL 60601
(312) 263-0456

North Central Association of Colleges and Schools Commission
   on Schools
Arizona State University
Temple, AZ 85287-3011
(800) 525-9517

Northwest Association of Schools and Colleges Commission
   on Colleges
3700-B University Way, NE
Seattle, WA 98105
(206) 543-0195

Southern Association on Colleges and Schools Commission on
    Colleges and Commission on Occupational Education Institutions
1866 Southern Lane
Decatur, GA 30033-4097
(800) 248-7701

Western Association of Schools and Colleges Accrediting
    Commission for Senior Colleges and Universities
c/o Mills College, Box 9990
Oakland, CA 94613
(415) 632-5000

Western Association of Schools and Colleges Accrediting
    Commission for Community and Junior Colleges
3060 Valencia Avenue, Suite 3
Aptos, CA 95003
(408) 688-7575

Western Association of Schools and Colleges Accrediting
    Commission for Schools
1606 Rollins Road
Burlingame, CA 90410
(415) 697-7711

National Institutional and Specialized Accrediting Associations
Accreditation Board for Engineering and Technology, Inc.
(212)705-7685

Accrediting Bureau of Health Education Schools
(219)293-0124

Accrediting Commission on Education for Health Services
    Administration
(703)524-0511

Accrediting Council for Continuing Education and Training
(804) 648-6742

Accrediting Council on Education in Journalism and Mass
    Communications
(913) 864-3973

American Academy of Microbiology
(202) 737-3600

American Assembly of Collegiate Schools of Business
(314) 872-8481

American Association for Marriage and Family Therapy
(202) 429-1825

American Association of Bible Colleges
(501) 521-8164

American Association of Nurse Anesthetists
(708) 692-7050

American Bar Association
(317) 274-8071

American Board of Funeral Service Education
(207) 829-5715

American College of Nurse-Midwives
(203) 737-2338

American Council for Construction Education
(318) 323-2413

American Council on Pharmaceutical Education
(312) 664-3575

American Culinary Federation Educational Institute
(301)268-5659

American Dental Association
(312) 440-2500

American Dietetic Association, Department of Education
(312) 899-0040

American Library Association
(312) 944-6780

American Medical Association and Association of American Medical
Colleges-Liaison Committee on Medical Education
(312) 464-4657

American Medical Association-Committee on Allied Health
Education and Accreditation
(312) 464-4660

American Optometric Association
(314) 991-4100

American Osteopathic Association
(312) 280-5800

American Physical Therapy Association
(703) 684-2782

American Podiatric Medical Association
(301) 571-9200

American Psychological Association
(202) 955-7671

American Society of Landscape Architects
(202) 686-2752

American Speech-Language-Hearing Association
(301) 897-5700

American Veterinary Medical Association
(312) 885-8070

Association for Clinical Pastoral Education, Inc.
(404) 320-1472

Association of Advanced Rabbinical and Talmudic Schools
(212) 477-0950

Association of Theological Schools in the United States and Canada
(412) 788-6505

Career College Association-Accrediting Commission for Independent
   Colleges and Schools
(202) 336-6700

Career College Association-Accrediting Commission for Trade
   and Technical Schools
(202) 336-6700

Commission on Opticianry Accreditation
(301) 459-8075

Computing Sciences Accreditation Board, Inc.
(203) 975-1117

Council on Chiropractic Education
(515) 226-9001

Council on Education for Public Health
(202) 789-1050

Council on Naturopathic Medical Education
(206) 485-2063

Council on Social Work Education
(703) 683-8080

Foundation for Interior Design Education Research
(616) 458-0400

National Accreditation Commission for Schools and Colleges
   of Acupuncture and Oriental Medicine
(202) 265-3370

National Accreditation Council for Agencies Serving the Blind
   and Visually Handicapped
(212) 779-8080

National Accrediting Commission of Cosmetology Arts and Sciences
(703) 527-7600

National Architectural Accrediting Board, Inc.
(202) 783-2007

National Association of Industrial Technology
(313) 677-0720

National Association of Schools of Art and Design
(703) 437-0700

National Association of Schools of Dance
(703) 437-0700

National Association of Schools of Music
(703) 437-0700

National Association of Schools of Theatre
(703) 437-0700

National Council for Accreditation of Teacher Education
(202) 466-7496

National Home Study Council
(202) 234-5100

National League for Nursing, Inc.
(800) 669-1656

New York State Board of Regents-State Education Department
(518) 457-3300

Society of American Foresters
(301) 897-8720

Straight Chiropractic Academic Standards Association, Inc.
(803) 578-8770

United States Catholic Conference
(314) 427-2500

Appendix D

Major Active-Duty CONUS Education Centers

Alabama

Anniston
Army Education Center
ATZN DP EC
5th Ave., Bldg. 328
Ft. McClellan, AL 36205-5000
DSN: 865-3562/5263
CML: (205) 848-3562/5263
Service: Army

Fort Rucker
Army Education Center
ATZQ DPT E
Bldg. 5009, Andrews Ave.
Ft. Rucker, AL 36362-5122
DSN: 558-4695/3651
CML: (205) 255-4695/3651
Service: Army

Mobile
Commanding Officer
USCG Aviation Training Center
Education Office
Mobile, AL 36608-9682
DSN: 436-3635
CML: (205) 639-6427/3635
Service: Coast Guard

Commander
USCG Group Education Office
South Broad St., Bldg. 101
Mobile, AL 36615-1390
CML: (205) 441-6001/6022
Service: Coast Guard

Montgomery
Education Services
502 MSSQ MSE
221 Shumacher Ave.
East
Maxwell AFB, AL 36112-6218
DSN: 493-5959
CML: (205) 953-5959
Service: Air Force

Education Services
502 MSSQ MSE-G
100 South Turner Blvd.
Bldg. 826
Maxwell Gunter Anx, AL 36114
DSN: 596-4488
CML: (205) 416-4488
Service: Air Force

Redstone
Army Education Center
AMSMI PT ED E
Bldg. 3222
Redstone Arsenal, AL 35898-
    5192
DSN: 746-9761
CML: (205) 876-9761
Service: Army

Arizona

Fort Huachuca
Commander U.S. Army Garrison
ATZS HRH E
Bldg. 21112
Ft. Huachuca, AZ 85613-6000
DSN: 821-3010
CML: (602) 533-3010
Service: Army

Glendale
Education Officer
58 MSSQ MSE
7383 North Litchfield Park Rd.
Luke AFB, AZ 85309-1534
DSN: 853-7722
CML: (602) 856-7722
Service: Air Force

Tucson
Education Officer
355 MSSQ/MSE
5260 East Granite St.
Davis Monthan AFB, AZ 85707-
    5000
DSN: 361-4813/3812
CML: (602) 750-4813
Service: Air Force

Yuma
Commander
U.S. Army Proving Ground
Attn: STEYP MUR ED
Bldg. 501
Yuma, AZ 85365-9111
DSN: 899-2437
CML: (602) 328-2437
Service: Army

Marine Corps Air Station
Educ. Ctr., Box 99134
Yuma, AZ 85369-9134
DSN: 951-3589
CML: (602) 341-3589
Service: Marine Corps

Arkansas

Little Rock
Education Office
314 MSSQ/MSE
3510 Leadership Cir.
Little Rock, AR 72099-5034
DSN: 731-3417
Service: Air Force

California

29 Palms
Commanding General
Manpower Educ., Box 788102
MC Air Ground Combat Ctr.
29 Palms, CA 92278-8102
DSN: 957-6881/6085
CML: (619) 368-6881/6085
Service: Marine Corps

Alameda
Maintenance & Logistics PP
Coast Guard Island
Educ. Ofc., Bldg. 503
Alameda, CA 94501
CML: (510) 437-3941
Service: Coast Guard

Commanding Officer
Navy Campus Office
NAS 250 Mall Sq.
Alameda, CA 94501-5025
DSN: 993-2638/2639
CML: (510) 263-2638/2639
Service: Navy

Barstow
Education Office
Marine Corps Log. Base B203
Barstow, CA 92311-5011
DSN: 282-6118
CML: (619) 577-6118
Service: Marine Corps

Human Resources Dev. Div.
AFZJ CPH T Bldg. 286
Fort Irwin, CA 92310-5000
DSN: 470-3458/3745
CML: (619) 386-4442/3745
Service: Army

Camp Pendleton
Base Education Center
Bldg. 1331, Rm. 10
Marine Corps Base
Camp Pendleton, CA 92055-5001
DSN: 365-6593/6660
CML: (619) 725-6593/6660
Service: Marine Corps

Fairfield
Education Office
60 MSSQ MSE
530 Hickam Ave.
Travis AFB, CA 94535-2751
DSN: 837-3444
CML: (707) 424-3444
Service: Air Force

Ferndale
Naval Facility
Centerville Education Office
5228 Centerville Rd.
Ferndale, CA 95536
DSN: 730-3381
CML: (707) 786-9531, ext. 267
Service: Navy

Herlong
Commander
Army Educ. Ctr.
Sierra Army Depot SDSSI ACES
Herlong, CA 96113-5120
DSN: 855-4628
CML: (916) 827-4628
Service: Army

Lancaster
Commander
650 ABW/MSUE
140 Methusa Ave.
Edwards AFB, CA 93524-1400
DSN: 527-2713/4482
CML: (805) 277-2713
Service: Air Force

Lemoore
Navy Campus Office
Trng. Bldg. A, Wing 1, Rm. 108
Naval Air Station
Lemoore, CA 93246-5009
DSN: 949-3857
CML: (209) 998-3857
Service: Navy

Lompoc
Education Officer
30 MSSQ MSE
Bldg. 14001, 144 Wyoming Ave.
Vandenberg AFB, CA 93437-6312
DSN: 276-5933
CML: (805) 866-5933
Service: Air Force

Marysville
Education Office
9 MSSQ MSE
6399 C St.
Beale AFB, CA 95903-5000
DSN: 368-2525/2526
CML: (916) 634-2525/2526
Service: Air Force

McKinleyville
Education Officer USCG Group
Humboldt Bay
McKinleyville, CA 95521-9309
CML: (707) 839-6121
Service: Coast Guard

Oakland
Naval Hospital Education Office
8750 Mountain Blvd
Oakland, CA 94627
DSN: 828-5266
CML: (510) 633-5266
Service: Navy

Petaluma
Education Officer
USCG Training Center
599 Tomales Rd.
Petaluma, CA 94952-5000
CML: (707) 765-7012
Service: Coast Guard

Point Mugu
Navy Campus Office
Bldg. 164
Naval Air Weapons Station
Point Mugu, CA 93042
DSN: 351-8362/8457
CML: (805) 989-8362/8457
Service: Navy

Port Hueneme
Navy Campus Office
Naval Const. Bn. Ctr.
Bldg. 225, Rm. 110A
Port Hueneme, CA 93043
DSN: 551-3940
CML: (805) 982-3940
Service: Navy

Riverside
Commander
22 MSSQ MSE
1940 Graeber St.
March AFB, CA 92518-5000
DSN: 947-4441
CML: (714) 655-4441
Service: Air Force

Sacramento
Education Office 77 MSS DPEE
5146 Arnold Ave., Suite 2
McClellan AFB, CA 95652-1079
DSN: 633-4776/2227
CML: (916) 643-4776/2227
Service: Air Force

San Diego
Navy Campus Ashore
Bldg. 151, Box 222
Naval Station Code N262
San Diego, CA 92136-5222
DSN: 526-4920
CML: (619) 556-4920
Service: Navy

Navy Campus Office
Bldg. 7, ASW
San Diego, CA 92133-8600
DSN: 524-5531
CML: (619) 524-5531
Service: Navy

Navy Campus Office
Education Center
NAB Coronado, Bldg. 345
San Diego, CA 92155-5043
DSN: 577-2651
CML: (619) 437-2651
Service: Navy

Navy Campus Office
Bldg. 610 N, PO Box 357024
NAS North Island
San Diego, CA 92135-7024
DSN: 735-9589
CML: (619) 545-9589
Service: Navy

Navy Campus Office
Naval Submarine Base
140 Sylvester Rd., Bldg. 138
San Diego, CA 92106-3521
DSN: 533-7194/7195
CML: (619) 553-7194/7195
Service: Navy

Navy Campus Office
NAVSTA Treasure Island
768 H Ave
San Francisco, CA 94130-0768
DSN: 475-5511/5512
CML: (415) 395-5511/5512
Service: Navy

San Pedro
Commanding Officer
USCG Chase WHEC718
PO Box 3187
Terminal Island Station
San Pedro, CA 90731-0208
CML: (310) 514-6500
Service: Coast Guard

Santa Ana
Commanding General
Joint Education Center
MCAS El Toro
Santa Ana, CA 92709-5010
DSN: 997-2568
CML: (714) 726-2568
Service: Marine Corps

Sunnyvale
Navy Campus Office
Bldg. 25, Naval Air Station
Moffett Field, CA 94035-5103
DSN: 494-4995
CML: (415) 404-4995
Service: Navy

Colorado

Base Education Office
21 MSSQ MSE
301 W. Stewart St., Suite 106
Peterson AFB, CO 80914-1450
DSN: 834-4064/4879
CML: (719) 556-4066/4064/7738
Service: Air Force

Colorado Springs
Headquarters
USAFA Dept.
5136 Red Tail Dr., Suite N112
USAF Academy, CO 80840-2604
DSN: 259-3298
CML: (719) 472-3298
Service: Air Force

Fort Carson
Army Education Center
Bldg. 1117
Fort Carson, CO 80913-5049
DSN: 691-2124/2207
CML: (719) 526-2124
Service: Army

Connecticut

New London
Navy Campus Office
Naval Submarine Base
New London, Box 74
Groton, CT 06349-5074
DSN: 241-3335
CML: (203) 449-2672
Service: Navy

Delaware

Dover
Education Office
436 MSSQ MSE
520 13th St., Room 228
Dover AFB, DE 19902-6520
DSN: 445-4619
CML: (302) 677-4619
Service: Air Force

District of Columbia

Anacostia
Navy Campus Education Center
Bldg. 150, Nav. Sta. Anacostia
2701 S. Capitol St. SW
Washington, DC 20373-5821
DSN: 288-3615/1199
CML: (202) 433-1199
Service: Navy

Washington
Education Services Division
Walter Reed Army Medical
    Center
Bldg. 11, Delano Hall
6825 16th St. NW
Washington, DC 20307-5001
DSN: 291-2055/3187
CML: (202) 576-2682/3187
Service: Army

Education Office
89 MSSQ MSE
Stop 44, Bldg. 1413
Andrews AFB, DC 20331-5064
DSN: 858-6377
CML: (301) 981-6377
Service: Air Force

Education Office
1100 NCR SPTG DPE-B
114 Brookley Ave.
Washington, DC 20332-5114
DSN: 297-4110
CML: (202) 767-4110
Service: Air Force

Florida

Clearwater
Commanding Officer
USCG Air Station
Education Office
Clearwater, FL 34622
CML: (813) 535-1437 EXT: 321
Service: Coast Guard

Cocoa Beach
Education Officer
45 MSSQ MSE
1020 Central Ave., Suite 14
Patrick AFB, FL 32925
DSN: 854-2071
CML: (407) 494-2071
Service: Air Force

Jacksonville
Navy Campus Office
Box 157, Bldg. 199
NAS Cecil Field, FL 32215-0157
DSN: 860-5853
CML: (904) 778-5853
Service: Navy

Navy Campus Office
Yorktown St., Box 137
NAS Jacksonville, FL 32212-
    0137
DSN: 942-2475/2477
CML: (904) 772-2545
Service: Navy

Key West
Navy Campus Office
Bldg. A718, Box 9033
NAS Key West, FL 33040-9033
DSN: 483-2075/2408
CML: (305) 292-2075/2408
Service: Navy

Education Officer
16 MSSQ MSE
221 Lukasik Ave., Suite 1
Hurlburt Field, FL 32544-5411
DSN: 579-6724/6500
CML: (904) 884-6724/6500
Service: Air Force

Mayport
Navy Campus Office
Box 280015, Naval Station
Bldg. 460, Massey Ave.
Mayport, FL 32228-0015
DSN: 960-6341/6342
CML: (904) 270-6341/6342
Service: Navy

Miami
Education Officer
7th Coast Guard District
909 SE First Ave.
Federal Bldg., Rm. 532
Miami, FL 33131-3050
CML: (305) 536-7431
Service: Coast Guard

Miami Beach
Education Officer
USCG Valiant WMEC621
100 MacArthur Cswy
Miami Beach, FL 33139
CML: (305) 535-4373
Service: Coast Guard

Education Officer
Coast Guard Group Miami
100 MacArthur Cswy
Miami Beach, FL 33139
CML: (305) 535-4392
Service: Coast Guard

Opa Locka
USCG Air Station Miami
Opa Locka Airport Educ.
Opa Locka, FL 33054
DSN: 434-1190
CML: (305) 953-2113/2109
Service: Coast Guard

Orlando
Navy Campus Education Center
Bldg. 2036 NTC
1751 John Paul Jones Ave.
Orlando, FL 32813-8325
DSN: 791-4397
CML: (407) 646-4397
Service: Navy

Panama City
Education Officer
325 MSSQ MSE
921 Beacon Beach Rd.
Tyndall AFB, FL 32403
DSN: 523-4285
CML: (904) 283-4285
Service: Air Force

Education Office
USCGC Courageous WMEC622
Caller Box 2710
Panama City, FL 32402-2710
CML: (904) 233-3011/3033
Service: Coast Guard

Pensacola
Navy Campus Office
Program Manager
518 Turner St., Suite A
Pensacola, FL 32508-5227
DSN: 922-4510
CML: (904) 452-4510/2089
Service: Navy

Tampa
Education Office
56 MSSQ MSE
8208 Hangar Loop Dr., Suite 7
MacDill AFB, FL 33621-5502
DSN: 968-3115/3118
CML: (813) 830-3115
Service: Air Force

Valpariso
Education Office
646 MSSQ MSUE
502 West D Ave., Suite 100
Eglin AFB, FL 32542-6838
DSN: 872-8141/4529
CML: (904) 882-8141/43/4529
Service: Air Force

Georgia

Albany
Commanding General
Base Education Office
Marine Corps Logistics Base
Albany, GA 31704-1128
DSN: 567-5276
CML: (912) 439-5276
Service: Marine Corps

Atlanta
Commander ACES
Army Education Center
Bldg. 179
Fort McPherson, GA 30330-5000
DSN: 572-3852
CML: (404) 752-2268
Service: Army

Augusta
Education & Career Dev. Div.
ATZH HRE T Bldg. 40707
Fort Gordon, GA 30905-5020
DSN: 780-2103/2805
CML: (706) 791-2103/2805
Service: Army

Columbus
HQ USA Infantry Center
Educ. Dev. Div.
Fort Benning, GA 31905
DSN: 784-1716/2674
CML: (404) 544-1716
Service: Army

Hinesville
Army Education Center
Bldg. 130
HQ 3rd Infantry Division
Fort Stewart, GA 31314-5144
DSN: 870-8331
CML: (912) 767-8331
Service: Army

Kings Bay
Navy Campus Education Center
USS James Madison Rd.
Bldg. 1030
Kings Bay, GA 31547-2538
DSN: 573-4527/4574
CML: (912) 673-4527
Service: Navy

Savannah
Army Education Center
AFZP PAP ED H EDUC BR
Hunter Army Airfield
Bldg. 1290
Savannah, GA 31409-5011
DSN: 971-6130
CML: (912) 352-6130
Service: Army

Valdosta
Education Office
347 MSS MSE
3010 Robinson Road
Moody AFB, GA 31699-1518
DSN: 460-3150/3884
CML: (912) 333-3150/3483/3884
Service: Air Force

Warner Robins
Commander WR ALC/DPUE
620 Ninth St., Suite 217
Robins AFB, GA 31098
DSN: 468-3965
CML: (912) 926-3965
Service: Air Force

Idaho

Mountain Home
Commander
366 MSSQ MSE
635 Falcon St.
Mountain Home AFB, ID 83648-
    5115
DSN: 728-6363
CML: (208) 828-6363/6262
Service: Air Force

Illinois

Belleville
Education Office
375 MSSQ MSE
607 Pierce St.
Bldg. 3190, Rm. 111
Scott AFB, IL 62225-5421
DSN: 576-3327/3328
CML: (618) 256-3327
Service: Air Force

Granite City
Army Education Center
SAVAS CE Bldg. 108
Charles Melvin Price Ctr.
Granite City, IL 62040-1801
DSN: 892-4305/4359
CML: (618) 452-4305
Service: Army

Great Lakes
Navy Campus Office
NTC Bldg. 2
NTC Great Lakes, IL 60088-5100
DSN: 792-4681
CML: (708) 688-4681
Service: Navy

Iowa

Keokuk
U.S. Coast Guard Group
Upper Mississippi River
221 Mississippi Dr.
Keokuk, IA 52632-4219
CML: (319) 524-7511
Service: Coast Guard

Kansas

Junction City
Education Div. DPCA
1st Inf. Div. M Ft. Riley
Bldg. 217
Fort Riley, KS 66442-6824
DSN: 856-6481
CML: (913) 239-6481
Service: Army

Leavenworth
Commander
Army Education Center
Bldg. 74 ATZL GCT E
Ft. Leavenworth, KS 66027-5090
DSN: 552-2496/4181
CML: (913) 684-2496/4181
Service: Army

Wichita
Education Office
384 MSSQ/MSE Bldg. 312
McConnell AFB, KS 67221-5000
DSN: 743-4240
CML: (316) 652-4240/4243
Service: Air Force

Kentucky

Fort Knox
Army Education Center G3
Dir. Plans Trng. Mobilization
ATZK PTC T Bldg. 1174
Fort Knox, KY 40121-5000
DSN: 464-2834/7517
CML: (502) 624-4136/2427
Service: Army

Frankfort
Education Division
Bldg. 2135 AFZB PA ED
12th & Indiana
Ft. Campbell, KY 42223-5000
DSN: 635-2662/3402
CML: (502) 798-2662/3402
Service: Army

Louisiana
Leesville
Army Education Center
HQ JRTC & Fort Polk
Bldg. 7801 AFZX PA E
Fort Polk, LA 71459-6950
DSN: 863-5401/5732
CML: (318) 531-5732/5575
Service: Army

New Orleans
Navy Campus Office
NSA Bldg. 603 1A, Rm. 113
4400 Dauphine St.
New Orleans, LA 70146
DSN: 363-5159
CML: (504) 948-5159
Service: Navy

Shreveport
Education Officer
2 MSSQ MSE
723 Doohet Dr.
Barksdale AFB, LA 71110-2429
DSN: 781-2615
CML: (318) 456-2615
Service: Air Force

Maine
Brunswick
Navy Campus Office
Box 56, 1000 Burbank Ave.
Naval Air Station
Brunswick, ME 04011
DSN: 476-2122
CML: (207) 921-2122
Service: Navy

Southwest Harbor
U.S. Coast Guard
Training Officer
Clark Point Rd.
Southwest Harbor, ME 04679-5000
CML: (207) 244-4200/4212
Service: Coast Guard

Maryland
Aberdeen Proving Ground
Army Education Center
STEAP PA E Bldg. 3145
Aberdeen Proving Ground, MD 21005-5001
DSN: 298-3385/2518
CML: (410) 278-3385/2380
Service: Army

Annapolis
Personnel Support AC
Education Officer
Hospital Bldg.
U.S. Naval Academy
Annapolis, MD 21402-5051
DSN: 281-2033
CML: (301) 267-2033
Service: Navy

Cascade
HQ USAG Ft. Ritchie
ASQNJ P ED Bldg. 337
Ft. Ritchie, MD 21719-5010
DSN: 277-5843/4178
CML: (301) 878-5843/4178
Service: Army

Frederick
Army Education Center
1520 Freedman Dr., Fort Detrick
Frederick, MD 21702-5000
DSN: 343-2854
CML: (301) 619-2854
Service: Army

Ft. Meade
Army Education Center
AFKA ZI PA ED Bldg. 8452
Ft. Meade, MD 20755-5093
DSN: 923-6421
CML: (301) 677-6421
Service: Army

Odenton
Air Force Education Center
DET 2 1100 NCR SPTG/DPE
Bldg. 9805, Rm. 220
Ft. Meade, MD 20755-5260
DSN: 923-3352/3354
CML: (301) 677-3352/3354
Service: Air Force

Patuxent River
Navy Education Center
22192 Cedar Point Rd.
NAWC AD
Patuxent River, MD 20670
DSN: 342-4655
CML: (301) 342-4655
Service: Navy

Massachusetts
Bedford
Education Office ESC DPUE
29 Chennault St., Bldg. 1728
Hanscom AFB, MA 01731-1635
DSN: 478-2021
CML: (617) 377-2021
Service: Air Force

Boston
Commanding Officer
USCGC Seneca WMEC906
427 Commercial St.
USCG Support Ctr.
Boston, MA 02109-1096
CML: (617) 223-3083
Service: Coast Guard

Cape Cod
Commanding Officer
Coast Guard Air Station
Cape Cod
Otis ANGB, MA 02542-5024
DSN: 557-6440/6442
CML: (508) 968-6440/6442
Service: Coast Guard

Woods Hole
Commander
USCG Group Education Office
Woods Hole, MA 02543
CML: (508) 457-3227
Service: Coast Guard

Michigan

Charlevoix
Commanding Officer
USCGC Acacia WLB406
City Dock
Charlevoix, MI 49720
CML: (616) 547-5648/4447
Service: Coast Guard

Grand Haven
Education Officer
U.S. Coast Guard Group
650 Harbor Ave.
Grand Haven, MI 49417
CML: (616) 847-4505
Service: Coast Guard

Port Huron
Commanding Officer
USCGC Bramble WLB392
PO Box 610786
Foot of Lincoln Ave.
Port Huron, MI 48060-0786
CML: (313) 982-2684/2686
Service: Coast Guard

Sault Ste. Marie
Commander USCG Group
Training Office
Sault Ste. Marie, MI 49783-9501
CML: (906) 635-3206/3217
Service: Coast Guard

Traverse City
Commanding Officer
USCG Air Station
Airport Access Rd.
Traverse City, MI 49684-3586
DSN: 889-3470/3471
CML: (616) 922-8230/8228
Service: Coast Guard

Minnesota

Education Officer
USCGC Sundew WLB404
1201 Minnesota Ave.
Duluth, MN 55802
CML: (218) 720-5461
Service: Coast Guard

Mississippi

Biloxi
Education Office
81 MSSQ MSE
500 Fisher St., Suite 217
Keesler AFB, MS 39534-2562
DSN: 597-2323/3274
CML: (601) 377-2323/3274
Service: Air Force

Navy Campus Office
4801 Marvin Shields Blvd.
Gulfport, MS 39501-5010
DSN: 868-2785
CML: (601) 871-2785
Service: Navy

Meridian
Navy Campus Office
1001 Rosenbaum Ave., Suite 13
Naval Air Station
Meridian, MS 39309
DSN: 637-2671
CML: (601) 679-2671
Service: Navy

Missouri

Knobnoster
Education Officer
509 MSSQ MSE
470 Vandenberg Ave., Suite 140
Whiteman AFB, MO 65305-5063
DSN: 975-3592/5755
CML: (816) 687-3592/5755
Service: Air Force

St. Louis
Second Coast Guard District
1222 Spruce St., Rm. 2, 102BJ
St. Louis, MO 63103-2832
CML: (314) 539-2653
Service: Coast Guard

Waynesville
Commander
Truman Education Center
Bldg. 499
Ft. Leonard Wood, MO 65473-5000
DSN: 581-2183
CML: (314) 596-0172
Service: Army

Montana

Great Falls
Education Office
341 MSS DPE
7521 4th Ave. North
Malmstrom AFB, MT 59402-7502
DSN: 632-3533/4675
CML: (406) 731-3533/4675
Service: Air Force

Nebraska

Omaha
Education Officer
55 MSS MSE Bldg. 301D
Offutt AFB, NE 68113-3214
DSN: 271-5716
CML: (402) 294-5716
Service: Air Force

Nevada

Fallon
Commanding Officer
Code 100 OEC Naval Air Station
Fallon, NV 89496-5000
DSN: 830-2622/2525
CML: (702) 426-2622/2525
Service: Navy

Las Vegas
Commander 554 MSSQ MSE
4475 England Ave., Suite 217
Nellis AFB, NV 89191-6525
DSN: 682-5280/9406
CML: (702) 652-5280
Service: Air Force

New Jersey

Red Bank
Army Education Center
AMSEL PT HRD ACES
Bldg. 918
Fort Monmouth, NJ 07703-5038
DSN: 992-6043/3006
CML: (908) 532-6043/3006
Service: Army

Wrightstown
Education Officer
438 MSSQ MSE
1911 East 4th St., Rm. 111
McGuire AFB, NJ 08641
DSN: 440-3019
CML: (609) 724-3019/2313
Service: Air Force

Army Education Center
G3 Bldg. 5403
1st St. and Delaware Ave.
Fort Dix, NJ 08640-5332
DSN: 944-4894/5001
CML: (609) 562-4894
Service: Army

New Mexico

Alamogordo
Education Officer
49 MSSQ MSE
681 Second St.
Holloman AFB, NM 88330-8060
DSN: 867-3971
CML: (505) 475-3971
Service: Air Force

Albuquerque
Education Officer
377 MSSQ MSE
1900 Wyoming Blvd. SE
Kirtland AFB, NM 87117-5604
DSN: 246-9933/8955
CML: (505) 846-9933/8955
Service: Air Force

Clovis
Commander
27 MSSQ MSE
Cannon AFB, NM 88103-5000
DSN: 681-4184
CML: (505) 784-4184
Service: Air Force

White Sands Missile Range
Army Education Center
STEWS DPE E Bldg. 464
White Sands Missile Range, NM
    88002-5034
DSN: 258-4646/4211
CML: (505) 678-4211
Service: Army

New York

Ballston Spa
Commanding Officer
Nuc. Pwr. Trng Unit
PO Box 300
Ballston Spa, NY 12020-0300
CML: (518) 884-1852
Service: Navy

Brooklyn
Army Education Center
NYAC & Fort Hamilton
Brooklyn, NY 11252-5190
DSN: 232-4819/4715
CML: (718) 630-4715
Service: Army

Fort Drum
Education Division
Army Education Center DPCA
Ft. Drum, NY 13602-5018
DSN: 341-5131/4964
CML: (315) 772-5131/4964
Service: Army

Governors Island
Commander PP
MLCLANT Bldg. 400
3rd Floor, Sec L2
Governors Island, NY 10004-
    5081
CML: (212) 668-6369
Service: Coast Guard

Moriches
Commander
Coast Guard Group Moriches
100 Moriches Island Rd.
East Moriches, NY 11940-9791
CML: (516) 395-4460
Service: Coast Guard

Scotia
Department of the Navy
Personnel Support ACT DET
1 Amsterdam Rd.
Scotia, NY 12302-9460
CML: (518) 382-0473
Service: Navy

West Point
Commander
Army Education Center MAPA A
West Point, NY 10996
DSN: 688-3360/3762
CML: (914) 938-3360/3762
Service: Army

North Carolina

Cherry Point
Director Training/Education
Joint Education Center
MCAS PSC 8019
Cherry Point, NC 28533-0019
DSN: 582-3500/4348
CML: (919) 466-3500/4348
Service: Marine Corps

Elizabeth City
Commanding Officer
U.S. Coast Guard
AVN Tech. Trng. Ctr.
Elizabeth City, NC 27909
CML: (919) 335-6146
Service: Coast Guard

Fayetteville
Education Officer
23 MSSQ MSE
384 Maynard St., Suite A
Pope AFB, NC 28308-2373
DSN: 486-4692/4693
CML: (919) 394-4692/4693
Service: Air Force

Fort Bragg
Army Education Center
AFZA PA ET Bldg. 1
3571 Knox & Randolph St.
Fort Bragg, NC 28307-5000
DSN: 236-8906
CML: (919) 396-8906
Service: Army

Goldsboro
Education Officer
4 MSSQ MSE
1290 Cannon Ave.
Seymour Johnson AFB, NC
27531
DSN: 488-5331
CML: (919) 736-5331
Service: Air Force

Jacksonville
Commanding General
BCEC Marine Corps Base
PSC Box 20004, Box 202
Camp Lejeune, NC 28542-5001
DSN: 484-5512/3091
CML: (919) 451-5512/3091
Service: Marine Corps

North Dakota

Grand Forks
Education Office
319 MSSQ MSE
344 6th Ave.
Grand Forks AFB, ND 58205-
6336
DSN: 362-3313/3316
CML: (701) 747-3313/3316
Service: Air Force

Lamoure
Education Office
USCG Omega Station
RR 3, Box 91A
Lamoure, ND 58458-9098
CML: (701) 883-5227
Service: Coast Guard

Minot
Education Office 5 MSS MSE
210 Missile Ave., Unit 2
Minot AFB, ND 58705-5026
DSN: 453-2772
CML: (701) 723-2772
Service: Air Force

New England
Commander
DET 19 1 CEVG
Education Office
New England, ND 58647-9613
DSN: 675-5207
CML: (701) 579-4664
Service: Air Force

Ohio

Dayton
Education Officer
645 MSSQ MSUEE
2000 Allbrook Dr., Suite 3, Rm.
 18
Wright-Patterson AFB, OH
 45433
DSN: 787-2936
CML: (513) 257-2936
Service: Air Force

Toledo
Coast Guard MSO
Federal Bldg., Rm. 501
234 Summit St.
Toledo, OH 43604-1590
CML: (419) 259-6372/6395
Service: Coast Guard

Oklahoma

Altus
Education Officer
97 MSSQ MSE
316 N 6th St., Bldg 155
Altus AFB, OK 73523-5013
DSN: 866-6619/6100
CML: (405) 481-6619/6100
Service: Air Force

Enid
Education Officer
71 MSSQ MSE
446 McAffrey Ave., Suite 6
Vance AFB, OK 73705-5711
DSN: 940-7291
CML: (405) 249-7291
Service: Air Force

Lawton
Dir. Plans Trng. Mobilization
ATZR TD ED
CDR USAFACES
Fort Sill, OK 73503-5100
DSN: 639-3201/6344
CML: (405) 442-3201/6344
Service: Army

Oklahoma City
Education Office
OC ALC DUPE
7751 1st St., Suite 105
Tinker AFB, OK 73145-9148
DSN: 339-7408
CML: (405) 739-7408
Service: Air Force

Commanding Officer
USCG Institute CG AS1
PO Substation 18
Oklahoma City, OK 73169-6999
CML: (405) 680-3416/7283
Service: Coast Guard

Oregon

North Bend
Commander USCG Group
2000 Connecticut Ave
North Bend, OR 97459-2399
CML: (503) 756-9259/9245
Service: Coast Guard

Warrenton
Education Office
USCG Group Astoria
2185 SE 12th Pl.
Warrenton, OR 97146-9693
DSN: 891-3051
CML: (503) 861-6235
Service: Coast Guard

Education Officer
USCGC Resolute WMEC 620
Coast Guard Group
Warrenton, OR 97146
CML: (503) 325-7213/7214
Service: Coast Guard

Pennsylvania

Carlisle
Army Continuing Education Center
609 Butler Rd.
Carlisle, PA 17013-5017
DSN: 242-3943/4783
CML: (717) 245-3943
Service: Army

Rhode Island

Newport
Navy Campus Office
Navy Educ.Trng. Ctr.
61 Capodammo Dr.
Newport, RI 02841-1522
DSN: 948-3030
CML: (401) 841-3030
Service: Navy

South Carolina

Beaufort
Commanding Officer
Marine Corps Air Station
Joint Education Center
Beaufort, SC 29904-5010
DSN: 832-7484/7486
CML: (803) 522-7484/7486
Service: Marine Corps

Charleston
Education Services
437 MSSQ MSE
101 East Hill Blvd.
Bldg. 503, Rm. 211
Charleston AFB, SC 29404-5021
DSN: 673-4572/4575
CML: (803) 566-4572/4575
Service: Air Force

Commanding Officer
Navy Consolidated Brig
1050 Remount Rd., Bldg. 3107
Charleston, SC 29406
DSN: 563-1600
CML: (803) 743-0306, ext. 3100
Service: Navy

Naval Nuclear Power Training
  Unit
1260 Snow Pointe Rd.
Goose Creek, SC 29445-8612
DSN: 794-5946
CML: (803) 863-5946
Service: Navy

Columbia
Army Education Center
Imboden St., Bldg. 4600
Fort Jackson, SC 29207-5160
DSN: 734-5341
CML: (803) 751-5341
Service: Army

Sumter
Education Office
20 MSSQ MSE
420 Polifka Dr.
Shaw AFB, SC 29152-5000
DSN: 965-2148/2588
CML: (803) 668-2148/2588
Service: Air Force

South Dakota

Bell Fourche
Education Office
Detachment 21 ECRG
HCR 69, Box 139
Belle Fourche, SD 57717-8801
DSN: 675-2241
CML: (605) 385-2242
Service: Air Force

Rapid City
Education Officer
28 MSSQ MSE
1158 Ellsworth St., Bldg. 2405
Ellsworth AFB, SD 57706-4811
DSN: 675-2312/2310
CML: (605) 385-2312/2310
Service: Air Force

Tennessee

Millington
Navy Campus Office
7800 3rd Ave.
NSF Memphis
Millington, TN 38054
DSN: 966-5290
CML: (901) 874-5290
Service: Navy

Tullahoma
Education Office
656 SPTS DPU
100 Kindel Dr., Suite C205
Arnold AFS, TN 37389-3205
DSN: 340-5134/6886
CML: (615) 454-5134/6886
Service: Air Force

Texas

Abilene
Commander
96 MSSQ MSE
Dyess AFB, TX 79607-5000
DSN: 461-5539
CML: (915) 696-5539
Service: Air Force

Corpus Christi
Navy Campus Office
10461 "D" St., Suite 202
Corpus Christi, TX 78419-5018
DSN: 861-3236/3792
CML: (512) 939-3236
Service: Navy

Education Center
Bldg. 12, Rm. 104
Naval Air Station
Dallas, TX 75211-9501
DSN: 874-6615
CML: (214) 266-6615
Service: Navy

Del Rio
Education Officer
47 MSSQ MSE
635 5th St., Suite 4
Laughlin AFB, TX 78843-5257
DSN: 732-5520/5529
CML: (512) 298-5529/5520
Service: Air Force

El Paso
Education Center ATZC DPTM D
Bldg. 2912 USAADECENFB ED
Fort Bliss, TX 79916-6816
DSN: 978-6497/3363
CML: (915) 568-6497/3363
Service: Army

Army Education Center
Bldg. 11238, Box 8042
Biggs Field
Ft. Bliss, TX 79908-0042
DSN: 978-8909
CML: (915) 568-8035
Service: Army

Galena Park
Commanding Officer
USCG Marine Safety Officer
PO Box 446
Galena Park, TX 77547-0446
CML: (713) 671-5100, ext. 2370
Service: Coast Guard

Galveston
Commanding Officer
USCGC Dependable WMEC626
Box 1942
Galveston, TX 77553-1942
CML: (409) 766-5685
Service: Coast Guard

Greenville
Education Office
DET 2 645 MATS AFMC
PO Box 6056 CBN 029
Greenville, TX 75403-6056
DSN: 739-5606
CML: (903) 457-5686
Service: Air Force

Killeen
Commander
Army Education Center
Bldg. 211 AFZF PTM ED
Fort Hood, TX 76544-5056
DSN: 737-4432
CML: (817) 287-4432
Service: Army

Lubbock
Education Center
64 MSSQ MSE
230 I St., Suite 1
Reese AFB, TX 79489-5004
DSN: 838-3384
CML: (806) 885-3384
Service: Air Force

Port Arthur
Education Officer
U.S. Coast Guard MSO
2875 Jimmy Johnson Blvd.
Port Arthur, TX 77640
CML: (409) 723-6500/6525
Service: Coast Guard

San Angelo
Education Office
391 MSSQ MSE
281 Flightline Ave., Suite A
Goodfellow AFB, TX 76908-
3211
DSN: 477-3314
CML: (915) 654-3314
Service: Air Force

San Antonio
76 MSS/DPEE
312 Tinker Dr.
Kelly AFB, TX 78241-5902
DSN: 945-7317
CML: (210) 925-7317
Service: Air Force

Education Services
HSC DPUE
3105 North Rd., Suite B
Brooks AFB,TX 78235-5341
DSN: 240-3617
CML: (210) 536-3617
Service: Air Force

Army Education Center
Bldg. 2248 AFZG PA E
Fort Sam Houston, TX 78234-
5000
DSN: 471-2538/2409
CML: (210) 221-2538/2409
Service: Army

Education Office
394 MSSQ MSE
1760 Nellis St.
Lackland AFB, TX 78236-5542
DSN: 473-2895
CML: (210) 671-2895
Service: Air Force

Universal City
Education Services Ceter
12 MSSQ MSE
301 B St. West
Randolph AFB, TX 78150-4521
DSN: 487-5964
CML: (210) 652-5964
Service: Air Force

Wichita Falls
Education Officer
82 MSS DPE
426 5th Ave., Suite 4
Sheppard AFB, TX 76311-2928
DSN: 736-2811/6231
CML: (817) 676-2811/4118
Service: Air Force

Utah

Dugway
Commander STEDP PT E
USA Dugway Proving Ground
Dugway, UT 84022-5000
DSN: 789-3348
CML: (801) 831-3348
Service: Army

Ogden
Education Officer 75 MSS DPEE
7290 8th St.
Hill AFB, UT 84056-5003
DSN: 777-2710
CML: (801) 777-2710
Service: Air Force

Virginia

Alexandria
Army Education Center
8831 Farrar Rd.
Ft. Belvoir, VA 22060-5059
DSN: 656-5393
CML: (703) 806-5393
Service: Army

Arlington
Army Education Center ANPE
ED
Bldg. 219
Ft. Myer, VA 22211-5050
DSN: 226-3070
CML: (703) 696-3070
Service: Army

Education Office
Henderson Hall
HQTRS Battalion USMC
Arlington, VA 22214
DSN: 226-8205/8203
CML: (703) 746-8205/8203
Service: Marine Corps

Chesapeake
Naval Security Group Activity
1320 Northwest Blvd, Suite 100
Chesapeake, VA 23322-5000
DSN: 564-1336, ext. 8227
CML: (804) 421-8227
Service: Navy

Education Office
USCG Finance Center
1430A Kristina Way
Chesapeake, VA 23326
CML: (804) 523-6706
Service: Coast Guard

Fort Monroe
Army Education Center
Bldg. 96 ATZF PCE M
HQS Fort Monroe
Ft. Monroe, VA 23651-6546
DSN: 680-2454/4345
CML: (804) 727-2454/4345
Service: Army

Hampton
Education Services
1 MSSQ MSE
450 Weyland Rd.
Langley AFB, VA 23665-5715
DSN: 574-2962
CML: (804) 764-2962
Service: Air Force

Newport News
Commander
Army Education Center
Bldg. 1708
Fort Eustis, VA 23604-5214
DSN: 927-5508/3705
CML: (804) 878-5508
Service: Army

Norfolk
Navy Campus Afloat
Bldg. Z86
9370 Decatur Ave.
Norfolk, VA 23511-3499
DSN: 564-7020
CML: (757) 444-7020/7023
Service: Navy

Commanding Officer
Naval Brig Code 143
8521 Ingersoll St.
Norfolk, VA 23511-2699
DSN: 564-5601
CML: (804) 444-5601
Service: Navy

Navy Campus Office
Education Center
9269 First Ave.
NAS Norfolk, VA 23511-2398
DSN: 564-7090
CML: (757) 444-7090
Service: Navy

Navy Campus Education Center
1328 8th St., Bldg. 3005
NAVPHIBASE LCREEK
Norfolk, VA 23521-2434
DSN: 680-8279
CML: (757) 464-8279
Service: Navy

Petersburg
Army Education Center
Bldg. 11528
Ft. Lee, VA 23801-5120
DSN: 687-2605
CML: (804) 734-2605
Service: Army

Portsmouth
Education Officer
USCGC Forward WMEC911
4000 Coast Guard Blvd.
Portsmouth, VA 23703
CML: (757) 953-7853
Service: Coast Guard

Navy Campus Office
Education Center
Bldg. 272, Rm. 103, Naval Hospital
Portsmouth, VA 23708-5100
DSN: 564-0111, ext. 7853
CML: (757) 953-7853
Service: Navy

Education Office
USCGC Legare WMEC 912
4000 Coast Guard Blvd
Portsmouth, VA 23703
CML: (804) 483-8750
Service: Coast Guard

Quantico
Commanding General
Educ. Branch BRANCH MCCDC
3098 Range Road, Suite 102
Quantico, VA 22134-5126
DSN: 278-3308/4010
CML: (703) 640-3308/4010
Service: Marine Corps

Virginia Beach
Commander
Army Education Center
Bldg. 591
Fort Story, VA 23459-5068
DSN: 438-7151
CML: (804) 422-7151
Service: Army

Navy Campus Office
FLT Combat Trng. Ctr. Atlantic
Code 01Y
1912 Regulus
Virginia Beach, VA 23461
DSN: 433-6183
CML: (757) 433-6183
Service: Navy

Navy Campus Education Center
Bldg. 140, Rm. B112
NAS Oceana
Virginia Beach, VA 23460
DSN: 433-3129
CML: (757) 433-3129
Service: Navy

Washington

Bremerton
Navy Campus Office
385 Barclay St.
Bldg. 433
Puget Sound Naval Shipyard
Bremerton, WA 98314-5295
DSN: 439-4282
CML: (206) 476-4282
Service: Navy

Fairchild Air Force Base
Commander
92 MSSQ MSE
Bldg. 2365 Castle St.
Fairchild AFB, WA 99011-5000
DSN: 657-2340/2348
CML: (509) 247-2340
Service: Air Force

Oak Harbor
Navy Campus Office
Bldg. 126, Rm. 120
NAS Whidbey Island
Oak Harbor, WA 98278-1200
DSN: 820-2284
CML: (206) 257-2284/3357
Service: Navy

Port Angeles
Commander
USCG Group
Education Officer
Port Angeles, WA 98362-0159
DSN: 744-6431
CML: (206) 457-2213/2280
Service: Coast Guard

Seattle
Commanding Officer
USCG Support Center
1519 Alaskan Way South
Seattle, WA 98134
CML: (206) 286-9653
Service: Coast Guard

Silverdale
Navy Campus Office
Code 0024 NSG Bangor
1001 Tautog Circle Suite B
Silverdale, WA 98315
DSN: 744-6666
CML: (206) 396-6666
Service: Navy

Education Office
62 MSSQ MSE
132 3rd St.
McChord AFB, WA 98438-5975
DSN: 984-5695
CML: (206) 984-5695
Service: Air Force

Army Education Center
Bldg. 4248
Ft. Lewis, WA 98433-5000
DSN: 357-7174
CML: (206) 967-7174
Service: Army

Wisconsin

Milwaukee
Commander USCG Group
2420 S. Lincoln Memorial Dr.
Milwaukee, WI 53207-1997
CML: (414) 747-7120
Service: Coast Guard

Sparta
Commander Ft. McCoy
AFZR PAMP Adjutant Bldg. 1441
Sparta, WI 54656-5000
DSN: 280-4669
CML: (608) 388-4669
Service: Army

Wyoming

Cheyenne
Education Center
90 MSS MSE
7105 Alden Dr.
F. E. Warren AFB, WY 82005-3924
DSN: 481-3577/3759
CML: (307) 775-2117
Service: Air Force

Appendix E

Major Active-Duty OCONUS Education Centers

Alaska

Anchorage
Education and Training Flight
3 MSS DPE
21590 Lemon Ave., Suite 21
Elmendorf AFB, AK 99506-1400
DSN: (317) 552-2120
CML: (907) 552-2120
Service: Air Force

DPCA Education Division
6th Inf. Div. Light
USAG APVRPA AE
Bldg. 658, Rm. 132
Ft. Richardson, AK 99505-5100
DSN: (317) 384-0970
CML: (907) 384-0970/9068
Service: Army

Delta Junction
Army Education Center
501 2nd St. #6600
APVR FG PA E
APO AP 96508
DSN: (317) 363-1217
CML: (907) 873-1217/3269
Service: Army

Eielson
Education Services
354 MSS/DPE
3124 Walsh Ave.
Eielson AFB, AK 99702
DSN: (317) 377-5106
CML: (907) 377-5106/4193
Service: Air Force

Fairbanks
Army Education Center
AFVR FW PAED
1060 Gaffney Rd. #6600
Ft. Wainwright, AK 99703
DSN: (312) 353-7318
CML: (907) 353-7318
Service: Army

Homer
Commanding Officer
USCGC Sedge WLB402
PO Box 101
Homer, AK 99603-0101
CML: (907) 235-5233/5234/5235
Service: Coast Guard

Juneau
Commander APRU
17th Coast Guard District
PO Box 25517
Juneau, AK 99802-5517
DSN: (317) 388-2169
CML: (907) 463-2169
Service: Coast Guard

Ketchikan
Commander
U.S. Coast Guard Group
1300 Stedman St.
Ketchikan, AK 99901
CML: (907) 228-0227
Service: Coast Guard

Kodiak
U.S. Coast Guard
Education Center
PO Box 190033
Kodiak, AK 99619-0033
DSN: 487-5315/5119
CML: (907) 487-5315/5119
Service: Coast Guard

Commanding Officer
USCG Support Center
Box 14
Kodiak, AK 99619-5000
DSN: (317) 487-5761
CML: (907) 487-5761
Service: Coast Guard

Nome
Commanding Officer
USCG Loran Station
Port Clarence Box KPC
Nome, AK 99762-8998
CML: (907) 642-3844/3821
Service: Coast Guard

Sitka
Commanding Officer
USCG Air Station
611 Airport Rd., Box 65000
Sitka, AK 99835
CML: (907) 966-5579
Service: Coast Guard

St. Paul Island
Commanding Officer
USCG Loran Station
St. Paul Island, AK 99660-9998
DSN: 950-6461
CML: (907) 546-2384/2385/2386
Service: Coast Guard

Valdez
USCG Marine Safety Office
PO Box 486
Valdez, AK 99686-0486
DSN: (317) 950-3861
CML: (907) 835-4791
Service: Coast Guard

Australia

Alice Springs
Education Officer
DET 421 PACTOA
APO AP 96548
CML: 011-61-89-530633
Service: Air Force

Woomera
Education Office
5 SWS/CCT Unit 11014
APO AP 96552
DSN: 730-1350 Ext. 426
CML: 011-61-86-739426
Service: Air Force

Azores

Lajes Field
Education Services
65 MSSQ MSE Unit 6856
APO AE 09720
DSN: 314-535-5291/3375
CML: 011-351-9554-0100, ext. 5291
Service: Air Force

Bahrain

Education Services Officer
Admin. Supp. Unit PSC 451
Box 336
FPO AE 09834-2800
DSN: 318-439-4282/4088
CML: 011-973-4282/4088
Service: Navy

Belgium

Chievres
Education Center Shape
NSSG 80 ASG
CMR 451 Box 6629
APO AE 09708
DSN: 314-423-3466
CML: 011-32-65-443466/7
Service: Army

Cuba

Guantanamo
Navy Campus Education Office
U.S. Naval Station
PSC 1005 Box 424
FPO AE 09593-0028
DSN: 723-3960, ext. 4769
CML: 011-5399-2620
Service: Navy

Diego Garcia Island

Navy Campus Office
U.S. Navy Support Facility
Diego Garcia Box 60
FPO AP 96595-0060
DSN: 370-4100/4321
CML: 011-246-370-4321
Service: Navy

Egypt

El Gorah
Army Education Center
MFO LSU North Camp Sinai
Unit 31520
APO AE 09832
CML: 011-972-76281-801
Service: Army

Sharm El Sheikh (Sinai)
Army Education Center
South Camp MFO Unit 31530
APO AE 09833
DSN: 236-9303
CML: 011-972-76281-801
Service: Army

Germany

Ansbach
Army Education Center
Katterbach Heliport CMR 454
APO AE 09250
DSN: 314-467-2817/2730
CML: 011-49-9802-83-2817/2730
Service: Army

Augsburg
HC Cobb Ed. Trg. Testing
Unit 25001
APO AE 09178
DSN: 314-435-7511/6402
CML: 011-49-821-540-7511/6402
Service: Army

Babenhausen
Army Education Center Baben-
  hausen
CMR 462, Box 5280
APO AE 09089
DSN: 314-348-3656/3856
CML: 011-49-6073-38-656/856
Service: Army

Bamberg
Army Education Center
279 BSB Unit 27535
APO AE 09139
DSN: 314-469-7715
CML: 011-49-951-300-7715
Service: Army

Baumholder
Commander
22 BSB Baumholder
AETV BHR TE Unit 23746
Box 21
APO AE 09034-0012
DSN: 314-485-6408
CML: 011-49-6783-6-6408
Service: Army

Buedingen
Army Education Center
Armstrong BKS
414 BSB CMR 401, Bldg. 2225
APO AE 09076
DSN: 314-321-4736/4812
CML: 011-49-6042-80-736
Service: Army

Darmstadt
Army Education Center
Cambrai Fritsch Kaserne
APO AE 09175
DSN: 314-348-6116
CML: 011-49-6151-69-6116
Service: Army

Friedberg
Army Education Center
Unit 21104, Box 781
APO AE 09074
DSN: 314-324-3119
CML: 011-49-6031-81-3119/3529
Service: Army

Geilenkirchen
Education Center
470 ABF MSE
Unit 3485
APO AE 09104
DSN: 314-455-3715, ext. 235
CML: 011-49-2451-63-2244
Service: Air Force

Grafenwoehr
Army Education Center
Unit 28038
APO AE 09112
DSN: 314-476-2753/2653
CML: 011-49-9662-83-2753/2653
Service: Army

Army Education Center
Grafenwoehr Trng. Area
Unit 28130
APO AE 09114
DSN: 314-475-6219/7156
CML: 011-49-9641-83-6219/7156
Service: Army

Hanau
Army Education Center
Pioneer Kaserne
414 BSB Unit 20193
APO AE 09165-0012
DSN: 314-322-9600
CML: 011-49-6181-88-9600
Service: Army

Heidelberg
Army Education Center
Patton Barracks Unit 29354
APO AE 09014
DSN: 314-373-6176
CML: 011-49-6221-17-6176
Service: Army

Hohenfels
Army Education Center
Unit 28216
APO AE 09173
DSN: 314-466-2668
CML: 011-49-9472-83-2668
Service: Army

Illesheim
Army Education Center
Storck Barracks Illesheim
CMR 416 Box E
APO AE 09140
DSN: 314-467-4750
CML: 011-49-9841-83750
Service: Army

Kaefertal
Sullivan Education Center
293rd BSB Unit 29901, Box 5
APO AE 09086
DSN: 314-385-2053/3361
CML: 011-49-621-730-2053/3361
Service: Army

Kaiserslautern
Kleber Education Center
415th BSB
APO AE 09227
DSN: 314-483-8125/7204
CML: 011-49-631-411-8125/7204
Service: Army

Army Education Center
415th BSB Rhein Ordnance
  Barracks
APO AE 09227
DSN: 314-489-6283
CML: 011-49-631-536-6283
Service: Army

Kitzingen
Army Education Center
Unit 26124
APO AE 09031
DSN: 314-355-8743
CML: 011-49-9321-305-743
Service: Army

Army Education Center
Larson Barracks Unit 26512
APO AE 09225
DSN: 314-355-2651
CML: 011-49-9321-702-651
Service: Army

Kreuznach
Army Education Center
S2 3 410 BSB ACES Unit 24308
APO AE 09252
DSN: 314-490-6167
CML: 011-49-671-609-7266
Service: Army

Miesau
Army Education Center
Area Support Team Miseau
AERAS SM A
APO AE 09059
DSN: 314-486-3863
CML: 011-49-6372-86-3863
Service: Army

Ramstein
86 MSSQ/MSE
Unit 3220, Box 270
APO AE 09094
DSN: 314-480-2032
CML: 011-49-6371-47-2032
Service: Air Force

Sandhofen
Army Education Center
Coleman Barracks
Unit 30005, Box 56
APO AE 09166
DSN: 314-382-4235
CML: 011-49-0621-779-5276
Service: Army

Schweinfurt
Army Education Center
Conn Barracks CMR 464
APO AE 09226
DSN: 314-353-8308
CML: 011-49-9721-96-8308
Service: Army

Army Education Center
Ledward Barracks
CMR 457 280 BSB
APO AE 09033-0012
DSN: 314-354-6471
CML: 011-49-9721-96-6471
Service: Army

Schwetzingen
Army Education Center
Tompkins Barracks Unit 29058
APO AE 09081
DSN: 314-379-7696
CML: 011-49-6202-80-7696
Service: Army

Spangdahleim
Education Office
52 MSSQ MSE Unit 3655
Box 120
APO AE 09126
DSN: 314-452-6063
CML: 011-49-6565-61-6063
Service: Air Force

Stuttgart
Army Education Center
Panzer Kaserne
CMR 445
APO AE 09046
DSN: 314-431-2506
CML: 011-49-7031-15-506
Service: Army

Wiesbaden
Army Education Center
Wiesbaden Air Base
221 BSB Unit 29623
APO AE 09096
DSN: 314-337-5559
CML: 011-49-7031-15-506
Service: Army

Army Education Center
Giebelstadt Army Airfield
CMR 408
APO AE 09182
DSN: 314-350-6441
CML: 011-49-9334-87291
Service: Army

Guam

Education Services Officer
36 MSS/DPE Unit 14001
Box 14
APO AP 96543-4001
DSN: 315-366-2590
CML: 671-366-7232
Service: Air Force

Navy Campus Office
NAVCAMS Guam PSC 486
Box 142
FPO AP 96540-1838
DSN: 355-5554
CML: 671-355-5554
Service: Navy

Navy Campus Office
Naval Station Guam
PSC 455, Box 154
FPO AP 96540-1000
DSN: 339-6117
CML: 671-339-6117
Service: Navy

Hawaii

Aiea
Marine Corps Station
Base Education Office
Box 64130
Camp H. M. Smith, HI 96861-5010
CML: (808) 477-0412
Service: Marine Corps

Barbers Point
Navy Campus Office
Bldg. 50, 3rd Deck
NAS Barbers Point, HI 96862-5050
DSN: 684-3118
CML: (808) 684-3118
Service: Navy

Honolulu
Army Education Center
USCG Integrated Support Command
Honolulu, HI 96859-5000
CML: (808) 433-6366
Service: Army

Education Services
15 MSSQ MSE
900 Hanger Ave.
Hickam AFB, HI 96853-5246
DSN: (315) 449-8330
CML: (808) 449-8330
Service: Air Force

Navy Campus Office
NAVCAMS Eastpac
Honolulu Bldg. 63
Wahiawa, HI 96786-3050
DSN: 453-5241
CML: (808) 653-5241
Service: Navy

Kaneohe Bay
Joint Education Center
Marine Corps Air Station
Box 63077
Kaneohe Bay, HI 96863-3077
DSN: 457-1232/2158
CML: (808) 257-1232/2158
Service: Marine Corps

Monalula
Army Education Center
Fort Shafter
Bldg. T 320 Stop 410
Ft. Shafter, HI 96858-5003
DSN: 438-6105
CML: (808) 438-9217/9215
Service: Army

Pearl Harbor
Navy Campus Education Center
Naval Submarine Base
100 Nimitz St., Bldg. 584
Pearl Harbor, HI 96860-6500
DSN: 474-1278
CML: (808) 474-1278
Service: Navy

Wahiawa
Army Education Center
Bldg. 560, 2nd Floor
Schofield Bks, HI 96857-5003
DSN: 455-4986
CML: (808) 655-4986/0800
Service: Army

Iceland

Keflavik
Navy Campus Office
PSC 1003, PO Box 58
FPO AE 09728-0358
DSN: 314-450-6226/7795
CML: 011-354-25-6226
Service: Navy

Italy

Aviano
Education Center
31MSS DPE Unit 6125
Box 70
APO AE 09601
DSN: 314-632-7330
CML: 011-39-434-66-7330
Service: Air Force

Ghedi
Education Center
31 MUNSS DPE Unit 6345
APO AE 09610
DSN: 632-7424
CML: 011-39-434-66-7424
Service: Air Force

La Maddalena
Commanding Office
U. S. Naval Support Office
PSC 816 Box 1795
FPO AE 09612-0057
DSN: 314-623-8306
CML: 011-39-789-798-306
Service: Navy

Naples
Tri Service Education Center
PSC 813, Box 174
FPO AE 09620-0174
DSN: 314-625-4243
CML: 011-39-81-724-4243
Service: Navy

Sicily (Sigonella)
Navy Campus Office
U.S. Naval Air Station
PSC 812, Box 3090
FPO AE 09627-2680
DSN: 314-624-2519
CML: 011-39-95-86-2519
Service: Navy

Vicenza
Army Education Center
USASETAF ACES Unit 31401
APO AE 09630
DSN: 314-634-7698/7856
CML: 011-39-444-517698
Service: Army

Japan

Atsugi
Navy Campus Office
Naval Air Facility Atsugi
PSC 477, Box 5
FPO AP 96306-1205
DSN: 264-3280
CML: 011-81-3117-64-3280
Service: Navy

Honshu
Army Education Center
Academic Trng. Div. DSPO
17 Area Supp. Group Unit 45006
APO AP 96343-0064
DSN: 263-3031
CML: 011-81-3117-63-3031
Service: Army

Education Center
374 MSS DPE
Unit 5123
APO AP 96328
DSN: 315-225-7337
CML: 011-81-3117-55-7337
Service: Air Force

Iwakuni
U.S. Marine Corps
Joint Education Office
PSC 561, Box 791
FPO AP 96310-0791
DSN: 253-3855
CML: 011-81-6117-53-3855
Service: Marine Corps

Misawa
Base Education Center
35 MSS DPE Unit 5021
APO AP 96319-5021
DSN: 315-528-4201
CML: 011-81-3117-66-4201
Service: Air Force

Okinawa
Base Education Office
Marine Corps Base Camp Butler
Unit 35023
FPO AP 96373-5023
DSN: 635-3944/3486
CML: 011-81-611735-7160
Service: Marine Corps

Education Services
18 MSS DPE Unit 5134, Box 40
APO AP 96368-5134
DSN: 315-634-5946
CML: 011-81-6117-345946
Service: Air Force

Army Education Center
Torri Station APAJ GO SPO E
10ASG
Unit 35115
APO AP 96376-5115
DSN: 644-4301
CML: 011-81-61173-14301
Service: Army

Education Office
U.S. Naval Hospital
Okinawa, Japan PSC 492
FPO AP 96362-1600
DSN: 643-7562
CML: 011-81-611-743-7562
Service: Navy

Yokosuka
Navy Campus Office
U.S. Fleet Activities
PSC 473, Box 99
FPO AP 96349-3004
DSN: 234-5058
CML: 011-81-468-261911, ext.
5058
Service: Navy

Korea

Chunchon
Army Education Center
USAG Camp Page Unit 15002
APO AP 96208-0252
DSN: 315-721-5838/5839
CML: 011-82-361-59-5838/5839
Service: Army

Kunsan
Base Education Office
8 MSS DPE Unit 2102
APO AP 96264-2102
DSN: 315-782-5148
CML: 011-82-654-470-5148
Service: Air Force

Osan-Ni
Education Officer
51 MSS DPE
APO AP 96278-5000
DSN: 315-784-4220
CML: 011-82-333-661-4220
Service: Air Force

Pusan
Army Education Center
Camp Hialeah EANC PC P ED
Unit 15490
APO AP 96259-0558
DSN: 763-7516
CML: 011-82-051-801-7516
Service: Army

Pyongtaek
Army Education Center
Camp Hunphreys Unit 15592
APO AP 96271-0567
DSN: 315-753-8906
CML: 011-333-690-8904
Service: Army

Taegu
Army Education Center
20th Support Group Unit 15494
APO AP 96218-0562
DSN: 315-768-7919
Service: Army

Tonguchon-Ni
Army Education Center
East Camp Casey
501 Support Corp Group
Unit 15596
APO AP 96224-0308
DSN: 730-2645
CML: 315-730-2645
Service: Army

Army Education Center
2D BDE Camp Hovey Unit
   15058
APO AP 96224-0319
DSN: 315-730-5161/5162
CML: 011-82-351-60-5161/5162
Service: Army

Army Education Center
West Camp Casey Unit 15600
APO AP 96224-0572
DSN: 730-6859
CML: 315-730-6859
Service: Army

Uijongbu
Army Education Center
HQTRS 6th BN 37 FA
Camp Essayons Unit 15404
APO AP 96257-0224
DSN: 315-730-6390
CML: 02-351-870-6390
Service: Army

Army Education Center
Camp Red Cloud
Unit 15353
APO AP 96258-0076
DSN: 732-1112
CML: 011-82-351-732-60617
Service: Army

Army Education Center
Camp Stanley 2nd Div. Arty.
Unit 15565
APO AP 96257-0624
DSN: 315-730-1110
CML: 82-351-39-732-1541
Service: Army

Waegwan
Army Learning Center
Camp Carroll 20th Sup. Group
Unit 15476 EANC TW E
APO AP 96260-0546
DSN: 315-765-7702
CML: 011-82-545-970/7702
Service: Army

Wongju Kangwon-Do
Army Educaiton Center
Camp Long Sub Post Unit 15575
APO AP 96297-0634
DSN: 721-3425/3408
CML: 82-371-83-3425/3408
Service: Army

Yong-Tae-Ri
Army Education Center
Camp Howze Unit 15529
APO AP 96251-0595
DSN: 315-734-5261
CML: 011-82-348-940-5262
Service: Army

Army Education Center
Camp Greaves
1/506 INF BN 2 Div. Unit 15528
APO AP 96251-0594
DSN: 315-734-8498
Service: Army

Army Education Center
Camp Pelham 517 Cav. Unit
    15527
APO AP 96251-0593
DSN: 315-734-2427
CML: 011-82-348-50-2427
Service: Army

Yongsan
Army Education Center
34th Support Group EANC SA E
Unit 15556
APO AP 96205-0614
DSN: 723-4290
CML: 011-22-7913-4290
Service: Army

Kuwait

Doha
Education Center
Artas K Unit 69900
APO AE 09889-9900
DSN: 318-438-5094
CML: 011-965-487-8822,
ext. 5094
Service: Army

Netherlands

Brunssum
Army Education Center
254th BSB AFCENT Unit 21602
APO AE 09703
DSN: 314-360-1110
CML: 011-31-455239-708
Service: Army

Norway

Stavanger
Education Center
426 ABS DPE Unit 6655, Box 15
APO AE 09707-6655
DSN: 314-224-1437
CML: 011-47-5164-1437
Service: Air Force

Panama

Howard Air Force Base
Commander
24 MSSQ MSE Unit 0585
APO AA 34001-5000
DSN: 313-284-4863
CML: 011-507-84-4863/5706
Service: Air Force

Puerto Rico

Aguadilla
U.S. Coast Guard
Air Station Borinquen Ramey
Aguadilla, PR 00604
CML: (809) 882-3500 ext. 1008
Service: Coast Guard

Roosevelt Roads
Navy Campus Office
Box 3406, PSC 1008
FPO AA 34051-3406
DSN: 831-4052
CML: (787) 865-4052
Service: Navy

San Juan
Army Education Center
Bldg. 219, Crane Loop
Ft. Buchanan, PR 00934-5008
DSN: 740-3244/8278
CML: (787) 273-3244
Service: Army

Sebana Seca
Commanding Officer
U.S. Naval Security Group ACT
Sabana Seca, PR
FPO AA 34053
DSN: 831-7258
CML: (809) 795-2255 ext. 250
Service: Navy

Saudi Arabia

Dhahran
Education Center
ARCENT SA
APO AE 09894
DSN: 318-431-6043
CML: 011-966-3-899-1119-431-
6043
Service: Army

Army Education Center
4409 OSG MSE Unit 66203
APO AE 09852-6203
CML: 011-9661-498-8932
Service: Army

Spain

Rota
Navy Campus Office
PSC 819, Box 54
FPO AE 09645-0008
DSN: 314-727-2711
CML: 011-34-56-82-2711
Service: Navy

Thailand

Chiang Mai
Commander DET 415
American Embassy Box C
APO AP 96546-0002
CML: 011-66-53-217353
Service: Air Force

Turkey

Adana (Incirlik AB)
Education Office
39 MSSQ MSE Unit 7075
Box 160
APO AE 09824-5160
DSN: 314-676-3211/6434
CML: 011-90-322-316-3211
Service: Air Force

United Kingdom

England

Harrogate
Education Center
Menwith Hill Station
PSC 45 APO AE 09468
DSN: 314-282-7851
CML: 011-44-1423-77-7851
Service: Army

Lakenheath
Education Office
48 MSSQ MSE
Unit 5200, Box 100
APO AE 09464
DSN: 314-226-3851
CML: 011-44-1638-32-3851
Service: Air Force

London
Education Office
Comnavactuk
PSC 802, Box 74
FPO AE 09499-1000
DSN: 314-235-4273/4557
CML: 011-44-171-514-4273/4557
Service: Navy

Mildenhall
Education Officer
100 MSSQ MSET Unit 4925
Box 275
APO AE 09459
DSN: 314-238-2350
CML: 011-44-1638-54-2350
Service: Air Force

INDEX

NOTES

NOTES